THEY CALL YOU DOC

Short Stories of a Draftee

BY

Michael Schneider

Edited by Christine Znak

Handball Photo by permission and courtesy of Luis Santana's HB page on Facebook.

This Collection is Dedicated to My Mother and My Wife.

They are the ones who make all things possible.

Thanks also to my children who opened my heart.

With Remembrance of those Lost, They are with me.

Hope you like being with Us.

About the Author

Talkative and Friendly, Tall, with Big Shoulders, German/Irish, having all the blessings life can give, He loves to tell stories to anyone who will listen. Content and Grateful, he feels our shared experiences are important. Hoping that you agree and find much common ground.

The stories are shaped by Family Life in New York City, the Draft, Viet Nam, and finally Family LIfe back in NYC.

As of this writing, he is retired and engaged in the Handball Sport and Happy.

The stories are as true as I could make them. Names are altered.

Preface

They Call You, Doc'   1970 Manchu Infantry, West of Cu Chi

What a test for my muddled brain, it was the mind of a young American, all full of the hero legends and the turmoil of 1969. The idea of selflessly tending to the battlefield wounded, mixed with the demeaning status of draftee. The crazy position of not wanting to even be here, or involved in any way, and now being expected to brave anything for your troops. They are yours now; you can't deny it. You can be a crummy soldier, you can grumble about the lifers, you can skip walking the point, but when they call, "Hey, Doc'", well, that is you. You can worry about the future, you can get away with a lot of stuff, you're a privileged character. You can curse the VC, you can go ahead and kid around about being somewhere else when it hits, but, if they call your name, you will go. Your name is Doc'; they call you Doc' and they know that Doc' will come and get them, no matter what, no matter. The Army doesn't matter, nor the heat. The jungle isn't going to stop you and the firing will only make you crawl a little faster, or kill you. Whoever came up with this job description did it just to box me in.

You are in so deep because you live with these lives in your hands. It works on your mind. They remind you about it. They have created the person that you must now be. They ask, "Doc, you will get me, right ?" You extort them for the cocoa they just heated up over the C-4 from their Claymores. They say, "I am going to call real loud, Doc'" and you say "Don't give away my position." They never admit how much they believe in you, and you never stop teasing about just leaving them there until resupply comes with somebody new. You swear, in the end, that you will not move an inch unless they give you that water, that drink, that cake. I had become "Doc". Okay ! I could not get out of it. For me this meant tormenting everyone about what a lousy deal I had. What a nuisance I was, always saying that we would be wiped out and second-guessing the entire chain of command. I didn't feel bad about it: I was going to get killed for these guys, in this snake pit swamp of a war. So, they had to suffer. I always told everyone I met, "Don't let me get over on you " Fair warning. In a very schizoid way, I was completely commited, so to speak.

I certainly hoped that no troop of mine would ever need to call, at all. I mostly feared my fear, not for my safety, but for theirs. After I had heard the call and answered, the feelings were the same. Always the doubt about the fear. Every day is a new test, even today. The burden no longer existed as something outside of you. You are inside the reality of your name. And, In this serious world, they call you Doc'.

Chapter One: Golden Boy

Late Afternoons in 1956, That Little Bugger.

Lucky me, my Grandparents live upstairs from us, in our two family house. I'm just a tiny guy, so mostly my time is spent downstairs with my Mom. Of course, I always want to go upstairs with Grandma. There is nothing so desirable, as Grandma's house, to a little boy. She cooks pancakes, that she calls, Fannakukins. She loves little me, and also tries to make me behave. She was born in Ireland, as was my Grandpa, and used all kinds of expression combining English and Gaelic, with a pinch of naughtiness. She always said, "Adelbless", when I acted silly. She said, "Go ongo wally", when she laughed. Being around these two was just fascinating.

They watched Wrestling on TV, which was my Grandma's favorite, especially Arnold Skollan, "The Golden Boy". All the oldtime wrestlers were great to me. I liked Bruno Sammartino and Argentino Apollo, and We Hated Skull Murphy. The best part by far, was being on the couch with Grandma, who believed that wrestling was real. At six years old, I knew better.

My visiting hours were limited somewhat, by Grandpa. I am pretty sure he was not always a fan, of the Scootch, that was me. I really loved to "get a rise out of him" and would pester him any way I could. Of course, I was not too sophisticated in my tactics. Mostly, I just ran too close to his chair, or made too much noise. He would holler and make great threats, while almost coming after me. My Mom and Grandma would try to stop this with varied results anyway.

The very best of the Scootching was when Grandpa would come home from his trackman job on the Long Island Railroad. He wore overalls to work, walked home two miles each day, and expected to eat and rest when he arrived. I know he did not have eels, cause that was for breakfast. At this time each day, I would be banished to the downstairs, in our Mother/Daughter House. There was a door at the top of the staircase, and ours at the bottom. These would both start out closed.

Whatever went on Upstairs, would take enough time for me to be eager in the extreme, to get back up there! Mom would have been worn down keeping our door secure, and I would begin my slow creep up, to visit. This would always be too soon for Grandpa, ALWAYS. He would be finished with his meal, sitting in his chair, around to the right of the Upstairs door. The door was never open, as my scootchboy antics started. Quiet as can be, I climbed to the top landing. This fooled nobody. The last step was sideways, to the right, the doorknob being so high, I could hardly reach it alone. Here, I would exercise patience, listening for an "opening", so to speak. The six-year-old period of patience exists, for an instant.

Initiate step two. Making noise to give them a hint. Maybe, they didn't know I was waiting. No sense letting them make a mistake; they were probably looking for me to visit.

First contact would be tiny knocks. These would never seem to be heard. Next, some vocal cues, like a cat meow or the pretend whistle I was practicing. Building on these foundations was easy. Now, I just began the beg / knock phase, appealing to Grandma for salvation. I was probably hungry, thirsty, lonely, all manner of needy. She would quietly tell me, through the door, that Grandpa was resting, and come back in an hour. I stayed at the top of the stairs, waiting. This may have amounted to 30 seconds of silence. Now, I could inform Grandma that I was ready to visit, again. At this time, I may hear Grandpa's voice, sounding far away, though his chair was only eight feet away, in the east corner of their living room. Some bubbling form of happiness would begin to motivate my pestering, now. My gifted intelligence emerged in the form of efforts toward stimulating my nemesis to action. I would be consumed with this quest to aggravate my Grandpa into attack mode. He was all I feared and loved. He must have loved this, I hope.

Silence / Knock / Silence /Meow /Silence / "Grammmpaaa" / Silence / "Gram' --

"Michael, GET OFF those Stairs, before I come after you". Grandpa's hollering would send me bouncing down the stairs on my Adelbless". Grandma would open the door and tell me, "Go on Gowally"/

My Mom would now forbid me to sneak back up. Funny, though, BOTH of the doors would be left open and I always went back up to watch wrestling with my Grandparents and "The Golden Boy" A... double S, get it ? She was a church lady.

Chapter Two: Dad Goes to School

September, 1954   Holy Child Jesus School

Kindergarden, Sister Carole is my teacher. I have been in class for two weeks. She made me stop crying, by threatening to change my seat. If I can't sit next to my friend Ricky, this will be hell.

My Mom, always takes me there, everyday, for half a day, morning session. Sister Carole is so magnificently beautiful and otherworldly, in her black and white habit; the stiff paper bib she wears is bright as the lights above; her head comes up to a two tiered, pointy square. The thing surrounds her face and squeezes her cheeks, until they extend past the edges, like pie crust.

I, Love Sister Carole; she smells holy as hell, and is tall as the cabinets.

Today, my father is walking me to school; up 110th Street, we stride. My dad walks like General McArthur, only not so punky. He literally marches, with stiff shoulders and long steps. I am too little for marching songs, but HCJ school plays them when we file in from the line-up outside. They are all way too slow for walking with Dad, which you don't; you only try to catch up, and the little things you have for legs cannot quite make it. He works in a clothing store on 42nd street in "the city". He is always in a "Rogers Peet" suit, and I am in my short pants, the HCJ uniform. I feel about as big as a mail box and my lid is flapping louder.

We get there, and no other people are about in the yard, or by the entranceway on 86th Avenue. The line-up in the yard must be over, and I am, LATE!!! My Dad is upset, for sure, as am I. This is a matter of awful concern "Kindergarden Lateness". I am near tears, which means, I am crying steadily. My Dad brings me over to the doorway, and asks if this is where I go in. I know it is, but not ALONE !

Now, my Dad was in World War II; he is a man, OK, but. . . he sends me, up the one flight of stairs to my class, on my own. This Being one too many missions, I suppose, for this ex- 8th Airforce Flyer with a Distinquished Flying Cross Medal. Certainly says something about a woman in a uniform !

As I open the corridor door, my Dad is peeking up at me, God bless his courage. No sooner is this done, then Sister Carole stands before me. All eleven feet of her. She whisks me down the stairs to Dad, who is now caught in her thrall as well.

"Oh, Mister Schneider, Michael is a bit early today, you'll have to wait a few minutes to drop him off." Sister spoke as she walked right on by. The relief I felt was quite a new sensation. For Dad: Like landing back in England, I suppose.

Chapter Three: Stick Boats

May, 1957, Suddenly done, A very early memory of 110 TH Street.

I can go up to the Raulins' house. No further! No street, especially no street. OK, I am only seven years old. It has rained; water runs toward Atlantic Avenue, by the curb. By the Tiss' house I stand, on the curb - watching the water. Floating stick boats. Janet , Susan, Ray, all the little children, floating stick boats . The tree by the curb is wide and still wet, the life is shining.   Just nice.

Down the block comes, Ron. My age, Ron is a bit of a problem. Even at this young age, the order is set. Ron is outside. As if fated, he approaches, and begins to act irritating. He teases, first the girls, who I am in love with - and they are sisters- and they like me too! Then, he targets Ray who is little. Then Me. I am a child, but I am angry.

As I stand, facing the curb, Ron pretends to push me toward the puddles, and the street. I am NOT allowed to put one foot into that street. I say, "one push and I will punch you right in the face"... then he gives me - ONE PUSH, forward I go, one step, my foot in the puddle, my foot in the...Street ! I make, one turn, one turn and one swing, the right hand.

I see, One stunned face- Punched in the nose, full and blunt. Blood, tears, shock. Ron swears, I will be in terrible trouble. It would take three people, to contain all the reactions I was having !

The trouble came and went, but I never regretted that Stick Boat Day.

Chapter Four: Chasing Rosalie

September, 23, 1962 The Forest Park Section that is just behind Herman.

School just started, two weeks ago, but the seventh grade social scene is burning hot, considering the autumn weather setting in. The leaves are trying to turn a little early, and so are a lot of 12 year olds.

My friend Bucky says he is going back to play cocoa monster, at Forest Park after school today. Cocoa Monster is a fun tag game of " catch and hold", like Ring a leevio. I asked if I could go along, and Bucky wondered why I needed his OK. He was definitely a rung up the point ladder, as far as I was concerned, but didn't even know how much popularity he held. We were friends, since Kindergarden, so he said, "sure"; he would meet me up by the statue everyone called... Herman. Herman stood at the Southeast entrance to the Beautiful wooded area, called Forest Park. The square by Herman, was surrounded perfectly, by heavy bush that grew on rising slopes. Above the bush, all around, was a sidewalk border. In the center, a circle of concrete with four paths leading in the directions of the compass, defining four lawns. To the south corner, stood , Herman, a WW 1 monument of a ten foot tall doughboy, atop a noble eight foot pedestal. The plaque said it was a tribute from Richmond Hill to...Her Men.   Oh, the girls were playing. too. Thanks, Bucky

The game was a "Base" vs. "Runners" contest. Sort of a Jailbreak, in fact, some called it 'Jailbreak'. The beauty of this space was the defined borders, combined with the tunnel-like hatches and cuts through and under the bushes. This made for great chases and fun. Added benefit here would be catching your favorite girl and being out of sight. Mostly, it was a game of tag, with a side of "be my girlfriend."

The afternoon was magnificent, and cool enough to need a sweater or sweatshirt. If anyone was missing from the class, I didn't notice. All the best kids were there; in fact, they were there before me. This game was on day two, and yesterday had already begun making reputations.   Boys and Girls growing up, kind of sweet and innocent, yet a bit bawdy and dangerous.

Teams are made up quickly by two Captains, Bucky and Mikey. They choose big boys, friends, popular girls, easy and harmless; everyone is part of this group. There are no outsiders to be shunned, or picked last. I am a Jailer, a chaser. The runners bolt from the circle while we count to twenty. Some run and hide seriously; they have game plans. Others take two steps and dance about, taunting us. They are either crazy, fast, or have a Jail experience in mind. Some of the players are definitely going to get "Tagged". The idea is for us to jail all the runners, and win. They can free the jail, in the meantime, with daring runs into the middle. This game IS ring-a-leevio. Anyway, I am here for the game; off I go, chasing a few guys up and under the bushes. Lots of players are caught, jailed, and escape. Those in charge of guarding the jail are ensuring lawlessness reigns. I chase and lock up a couple of girls; they take it well, because we are friends. The game is lots of fun. Time outs, players loafing, talking, playing, and some pairs getting a kiss, or an embarassing clutch.

After running around fifteen minutes or so, my sights fall on a nice girl named Rosalie. She is so much like me that we have almost the same clothes on. Her braids are bouncing all over, as she runs away from me. We are playing tag, this is not the boy / girl event, I don'think. She can run and gets almost into the densest cover before I grab her and we crumble down. My breath is short, hers fast, as we gather ourselves. She is laughing, and looks so happy, as the day fades. I feel very exhilarated, staring at her wordlessly. Her giggles quieting, I see a look in her, that I like.

Just as we might... well, I am not sure; she sees a bunch of change in the grass. Lots of coins! We pick up a dollar's worth. Her attention shifted much faster than mine, cause << I was going to kiss her.

Chapter Five: Any Other Name

Holy Child of September, 1960

I am ten, I just started wearing glasses to school this year. I hate that.

School is strict, I am smart. This makes me "different". You desperately do not want to be, that. Everyone is wearing uniforms; long hair does not exist for boys, all of the girls wear the same shoes, bows, and clips. We try hard to have the same lunchbox and bookstraps. We study conformity.

People are Irish, or German / Irish, like me. Or they might be Polish; for sure, they come from Europe. That is the only other real continent. Columbus discovered all the acceptable ones. They have 'Negro' people in Jamaica, where my Mom goes shopping. We take the Atlantic Avenue bus to Gertz and Mays Department Stores. I got my glasses in a building across from the hardware store, on Sutphin Boulevard, where we waited for the bus when coming home. The display of knives in the window was almost more than I could bear. Man, I wanted that Bowie knife!

We had Italians; they were relatively new in Richmond Hill. My friends, some who moved here from Harlem were teaching me about prejudice. And the Italians were the least white people you could tolerate. They were almost Spanish, according to the color chart, where I was living. The place was White. The reason was obvious: we were the best. The rest of the world was a mix of huts and tee-pees. The heathens scalped people, or ate them. We either conquered them, or they worked for us, somewhere. They made inferior goods and had diseases; they did not have straight hair. There was nothing to think about ! Who the hell could live in Africa ? The animals were as bad as the people. South America has so many giant snakes, that it worried me in New York City. Eskimos, Incas, Ubangies, Forget Asia, crazy people, hanging off the side of the earth. Not our style. This brings me to Julius, my very good and funny friend . He was Virtually Thee Co-Best friend of Johnny and Me. Julius was a tiny guy who made us laugh, at the wrong times, constantly. My career as a problem in school was unrelated to Julius, but all the laughing did not help.

This very sunny afternoon, we three are riding our bikes, which are three speed racers, of course. Riding all the way up past White Hill. Julius lives up here; his family has got the money to have a big house, with property on the side. Johnny just moved up here, too. My family will not be moving to Richmond Hill North, any time soon. We have been playing outside of Julius' house, for a few days. His Mom is always around. She is very beautiful and fine. She speaks to us in a way that makes me and

Johnny answer in our best language and manners. Like, "Yes, we certainly are having a fine time, Mrs. Lara". She asked us in for a cold drink, and we entered into their living room. The furnishings are magnificent; forget about sitting down, I don't get near anything. I don't belong here, at all. So, I stand by the mantle over the real fireplace, and look at the pictures. I notice that some of the men have on white dress clothes, while others are too colorful. The next picture is one of Julius, with an inscription, below that said, "Darling Julio". JULIO ! I am, IN, a " Spanish House", Ai yi yi. Much to my credit, I resist panic. Julius is a good friend, yes, he is. In my ten-year-old way, I just ask him, "What is wrong with the name on your picture?" He explains, without any of the angry reaction expected that THEY made him write his name as Julius, at the Holy Child School, when we were in KIndergarden Together! His real name was not acceptable! NOT acceptable. I do not think I ever learned more from one thing, in my whole life, ever. I was on the wrong team.

There was something unacceptable. The prejudice that could do that, to my friend and his loving family, was deeply wrong, and this was revealed to me, in that moment.

Chapter Six: Gift of the Mike Eye

December 24, 1960 Jamaica Avenue.

New York City, at Christmas time. I am Eleven and a few days old.

At Three P.M., under the Elevated 'J' line train, the weather on this dark winter street was getting inside my coat. My tiny amount of money was very deep in my pocket. My Mother was on my mind, and Christmas was filling my heart. I needed that present, that "special one", that said everything about Mom, about Christmas, and about Love. This one should be all that and cost about $ 3.25.

The most logical place for my shopping was The Drug Store on One Hundred and Eleventh Street, the cabinet of watches and colognes always looked like it contained air from Christmas. The lighting and clever display backdrops were enough to enhance the contents, to dreamlike perfection. Like children will, I had an item in mind. The Timex " lady watch." Something that would look pretty and be useful; my Mom was a practical person. Perfume wouldn't please her at all. The little tiny price placards under each item, were a detail that I'd never noticed. Those big numbers should never fit on such little cards. The least expensive thing in the case was $ 11. 50 and Mom wouldn't like a glass reindeer, anyway. Out, onto the street, under the Station, went a desperate Mike. Jamaica Avenue had lots of small shops, so I had hopes of finding, "Just That Gift,"

Past the shoe store, and the hardware, over by One Hundred and Fourteenth Street, was the Five and Ten. The whole Christmas Razzamatazz of that place just deflated me. Buying tinsel and fake flowers is for babies, I wanted THE gift. So full of Christmas spirit was I, that the trains deafening roar, sounded festive. The passing cars and trucks didn't crowd me; they accompanied my elvish quest. The baby Jesus was about to be born in Bethlehem; in my mind the Nativity scene smelled like pine wreaths. I headed back towards Jerry's Store on One Hundred and Tenth street, thinking of how to make socks seem, Christmassy.

Here, I am pretty sure the Angels intervened, summoned by the towering amount of little boy halo, rising from my head. On, One Hundred and Twelfth Street , I met Mr. Blatz, the Organist from Holy Child School. I sang in the Choir there. I was pretty sure that Mr.Blatz was about 97 years old, minimum. He was in front of the Religious Article Store, a place full of statues and curios, of all sizes. To me, it seemed like a part of the church, I'd once visited the store with Mom, who also seemed like part of the church.

Mr. Blatz was closing up the store. As a choir member, you never spoke. The Sisters led you in, sat you down and ordered you, to stand and sing. It was not a democracy. Maybe, Mr. Blatz realized that my singing was responsible for about half of the boys input. Quite a few girls sang all the time, most of the boys would rather get smacked. He was closing up early and met me in the doorway, perhaps he could sense my situation; after all, he wasn't new. Asking me if I would like to look around, he stepped aside. The tiny store was a magical shire of figurines, and smelled of the church type incense. I blessed myself. Just In Case.

Without hesitation, my eyes fell on a beautifully painted , miniature statuette of Mary holding the baby Jesus. Without hesitation again, my mind knew this was "The Gift." Honestly, it was like me and Mom on a statue. I thought I was exactly like the baby Jesus. Let's face it. I still do.

No price tag or placard, so I asked, "How Much, Mr.Blatz." He answered, "Well, Michael, that one is, two dollars and fifty cents." In about fifteen seconds, I was out the door with my Madonna and child. What luck, the breeze on Jamaica Avenue was glistening with snow, the trains were passing overhead, in both directions, one pulling into the station with a screech, and one leaving with the slap of the couplers banging, Just more Happy Jingle bells to me. ME, straight on, right home to get some wrapping paper from my big sister. She wrapped it for me. She always did the wrapping and craft things that made everything better. Giving me a funny look, when she was prepping the paper, " Very nice, Michael," she said. The hours until Christmas morning were even slower than when I awaited only receiving gifts.

My Dad got his usual, Tie and Gloves. The four of us kids got an avalanche of toys. And Mom opened her " Gift." She certainly loved it and held it high. My little brother and sister had not even seen it, and as a testimonial to the perfection of this statue, they asked to play with it immediately, allowing my Mom to say that, "No one will be playing with this." Holding it aloft revealed a tiny tag, or sticker beneath. Mom looked at it, then at me. My big sister, also shared a glance with Mom. "Michael, this cost so much, Merry Christmas and Thank You", Mom said.

Merry, Merry Christmas, Mr. Blatz, I owe you fifteen dollars.

Chapter Seven: Revelation

Jamaica, The Jamaica Avenue in Jamaica. NYC 1959

Fourth Grade, Mike is Not Happy.

We do not have a car; we take the bus. The lousy bus, which is the 'stupid lousy' bus, to Jamaica, to go to the stinking , lousy, crummy, Eye Doctor. Because, I do not need glasses, only my dopey jerk of a Teacher, Sister Stephen Mora, Old Double Smack, thinks I do. Only the Eye Chart at school is too far away, cause I can see fine and dandy. I play ball, don't I ? I can cross the street, I know people, I can read better than anybody. I'm tough, I do not wear glasses.

My Mother thinks, we should have my eyes examined, so on the bus I am grumbling. Soon as I pass the eye test, I can look at the knife display in the window on Sutphin Boulevard, while we wait for the lousy bus back home. There is a Nedick's there, a great place for treats and Orange drinks that come in paper cylinders sitting in their frames. That could be nice, after this dumbbell eye test.

The Doctor's Office is up tubey stairs, just East and across the street from the tall, red building, by the bus stop. The Doc', he is a gentle fellow, with the hair on each side of his head, and the spectacles way down his nose. He never looks through them, making me think he is faking bad vision to sell more, or to make people feel better about their own broken eyeballs. Nothing could console me; if I had to wear glasses, my life would be over. The insults alone would make me so mad, I would want to fight with a fever and THEN, I would have to take them off. God Jesus, that might have me so angry that I'd be crying, before the fight even started. No worries though, I was strong about my eyes, not handicapped, never that.

The Doctor had a drop down, side swing, face covering gizmo made of cold metal and gears, with hundreds of round lens that flipped. Yes, he had that. You sat in a Deeply Cushioned Leather Chair, the kind that felt solid and chilly, and he slung that geary gizmo onto your face. Right away, he had you using one eye at a time, ruining my best two-eye lean and squint trick. Next he began that flip / pick routine, confusing my best guessing ideas with blurry images. The R looks like a P, then the Q or Z, and this or that, clearer or . . . my confidence was slipping and my eyes were wet, with eye sweat. The time was up for me the Doctor told my Mom; he had gotten the right prescription for me. We could pick out frames and they'd be ready in no time. I wasn't man enough to fight back. This horror was happening to ME.

Before I even got out of the chair, he asked me to sample my Prescription through the magic of his Apparatus. Through my strangled emotions, I agreed. Now, I was facing the window. My Mom, standing in front. He adjusted the lens for each side and brought the monstrosity to my nose. I could see Mom right away. She looked about the same. Then, I lengthened my gaze, peering out the window to the Nedick's Sign which looked quite different.

Worst of all, the building wall was no longer a red slab, not a blur of red, NO, it was BRICK, and I could see each one.

My eyes were sweating steadily and I was in no rush to re-emerge from behind the mask.

I was not happy, but I saw a new reality, and had to accept it. Red means Brick.

Chapter Eight: Uncle Punk

August Nineteen Sixty, Ten years old.

On the block, up the block, in the alley, between the O'Donies' and the Brooms' houses. We've been in the pool, the O's pool. It's cool to be invited to the big blue circle of fun with the boys and girls of 110th street. Ten kids, all of them little guys like me, no real world problems, just kid type action.

Of course, we are involved with ruining some part of each day; this is the way with young people and old. The world is full of unnecessary misery, created by accidental, or purposeful mischief.

Today, my boy Tanzy has been inciting violence. This he can do actively, or by clever childish subterfuge. He can hit you and laugh, hit you and make you hit someone else, or have someone hit you. You could always tangle with the Tanz, anytime; bad choice there! Today, he is insulting you, on behalf of others, like reverse charity. Example: "He said you're a punk!", "He can take you", "your sister, your mother". You know these are nothing but Tanzyquips: "If you don't do something about that, you are a punk", - over, and over. This is not new, the players are my friends from the block and we have lost this game before.

Usually, I am smart enough, and fighter enough, to avoid the actual fights. I've fought with everyone before; they cannot take me, I am not a punk. Fought with Tanz, too. Do not want that again, he liked it ! By the time you reach ten, most 110th street fights are done. They go the same way. Things are done, settled, and rematches are just cruelty. Tanzy insists on this bullying; he is a tough boy and can easily assault any target. Can find reason to behave often, as few behave, ever! Not just a bully, he's an instigator. Can and does create trouble, loving every result.

This day, as we exit the pool, I am the tool used to amuse, by my poison friend. We are friends, how ? We just are. I might be his best friend. Sadly, provoked by Tanz, Jackie wants a fight, another one, with me. Jackie cannot accept reality. Four years of fights, all the same: Jackie crying and me, disgusted. Childishly, we fight. Nothing makes for yelling like fights, and the alley is really loud. The girls and boys make noise until someone gets hurt. The fun part is over then.

The neighbor, Mr. Broom {Danny's dad}, comes off his back porch. He is a man, maybe a drunk MAN. He pulls Jackie off my leg, where he is doggedly hanging, and begins to loudly lecture us. He tells us to hold out a hand, in front of him, Yells, pretends to slap us. Scares the crap out of us. Jackie is crying, maybe me too. The kids are moving back, even Tanzy, pretty intense for a minute, then fuming out. Mr. Broom sends us out of the alley. At least Jackie and Tanz have lost interest in fighting. I do not like to beat people up more than once. Not many can push me around. There are few fights left for me on one ten. If I have to, I give way. I know my place - BUT WAIT!

I guess the O'Donies have an uncle visiting. He must be a little drunk, too. He is a man, but not an old man. The story of the fight and the crying has made him act. Up the front steps of the Broom' s house he goes.   Me and the kids are right next door on the stoop. He knocks hard on the door and out comes old man Broom, looking all red faced and lame. He starts to TALK ...NO WAY !

O'Donies' uncle drags him down the front steps, and throws him to the pavement! Man, he is fired up. I am scared, horrified. This is for real !

Then, old man Broom wouldn't get up. Of course, He's a Punk.

Can't say I wanted to see more action. Grownups are scary without being out of control, violent, and drunk. I learned a lot on 110 STREET.

Chapter Nine: Tommy & Joe

October, 2 1959, Down Another Street.

Kids live in bursts of light, like this trip home from school for Tommy and Joe.

Three O'clock and today is Friday. Getting released from Fifth Grade at Holy Child School, feels like bright, flashing smiles. Today would be a good day to 'take the long way home' for Tommy and Joe. The stifling discipline of Sister Bernadette only extended to 111th Street, never beyond the big houses, over toward 86 th Avenue. Big boys, like Tommy and Joe, always walked home alone/ together. That combination of independence and 'schoolie fish' traveling. Richmond Hill was a place where children could walk with their secret fears, and parents could allow it. The sun crackled on the west facing school steps, the metal hand rails were baked to pleasing warmth. The shuffle of the class, down these steps and to the corner, was more silent than usual. Sister had made the class retrace our steps on the Stairs, for laughing. Laughing was, 100% , devil sent. Half the children were dismissed down toward Jamaica Avenue, before the rest followed Sister up to the corner of 86th and 111th. There, they would be released. Super sadly, a few parents would be waiting there for their darlings.

Sister, gave a "Get you on Monday" stare, at Tommy and Joe, as they crossed 111th street., heading for 110th. They were damn well supposed to walk down 111th; she knew that. But, today was a day for Chestnuts, on 110th. Chestnuts were useless, fun nuggets of trouble. Spiny shells, smooth and deeply colored nuts inside. They caused Tommy and Joe to crave them, with their smell, along with the feel of the surfaces when they were busted out of their porcupine coats. The curved tops accenting the flattened bottoms. Each pod contained a pair, that shaped the other by growing in the space. In this way, Tommy and Joe were like Chestnuts, occupying the space left by the other, but quite separate.

They saw a the batch of Holy Child kids, who lived on the North side. Tommy could not stop yammering about how big Ronnie was, "mJeez, Joe, he's like a Gorilla." He is the toughest boy in the sixth; even Bennie Turano shuts up when Ronnie is around. That said it all about Ronnie, cause Bennie even talked back to the Sisters. They waved to Fifth and Fourth Graders, who knew that "T 'n J" were roaming. They got brave a few times, and walked all the way to Mary and Linda's house on 102nd Street. Tommy felt famous.

As they came to the bottom of the stone stairs, by 110th Street and 86th Ave.,. the Suggs family kids were at the top looking, 'In the Way'. There was their classmate, Ricky, and two girls. One a little one, and the other, the Sixth grader. Tommy knew them, and he had 'noticed' Elita, who was kind of 'grownup'. As Joe headed up the four old stairs, Ricky stood in his way. Pushing right on through, Joe began telling Tommy, what a punk this kid was, and how he 'wrestle holded him'. Joe and Ricky hated each other, but Tommy had no interest in that. The trouble was coming cause the sisters were not moving. Joe said, "Tommy, you should put him in a sleeper hold." Tommy had no intention of doing anything , except peeking at Elita. He was squirmy, as hell. Joe kept bugging. Little sister said something dopey; Elita looked straight at Tommy. He could not feel any more awkward, when Ricky pushed him, and his books fell to the floor. Tommy grabbed the kid's nice white uniform shirt and blue tie, and pulled a punch, wrap, headlock, onto Ricky, before the kid could move. Tommy had a nasty headlock, but his desire to fight with Ricky was at zero. He held tight, while Joe screamed, "Headlock ,Headlock, punch his face, Tommy." There was a moment when Ricky should give up. That would be OK with Tommy, but Joe kept on yelling and then. . . Elita jumped onto Tommy's back, wrapping her legs around him, and huffing on his neck. This was, ALL wrong. Her legs were bare flesh against him, as her checkered skirt rose, with her attack. She felt warm, and wriggled back and forth, making Tommy so confused that, he punched Ricky. Ricky cried, Tommy released him, Big sister jumped off. Over, in a flash.

Joe picked up Elita's lunchbox and threw it down. Tommy just...Hated Joe, for that. Ricky was still crying, as Tommy picked up his books. Looking at Elita didn't help, she was all flushed and super triumphant. Tommy was full of mixed up emotions.

Walking south toward the Chestnut trees, Tommy stared at the floor, he wanted no pods. It wasn't Friday; he wanted to be home. Then Joe, Numbskull Joe, says, "Tommy, when she was on your back, I could see her...underwear." " Good God, Joe, what did you tell me that for, why did you look at that? Oh, shut up, Joe", Tommy yipped.

Joe noticed how upset Tommy looked. He said, "Don't cry now, man, you banged them good. You won that fight." But, Tommy did cry, and he cried hard, though he didn't know why.

He did know that he needed a new best friend.

Chapter Ten: Branded

Branded !

April, 1958   Up The Block,   In the Lots.

I'm still a little kid, but I am trying not to be. Grown ups have all the stuff, and time goes pretty slow when you're eight years old. My friends on 110th Street have been 'Out' for some time. My begging has succeeded in getting me released, in a limited probationary way. The Block is the whole world, sort of, a flat earth existence, but plenty for my childish ways. I don't even smoke, at least not until today.

My Dad sure can smoke. He handles the butts like a Tobacco official. Holds those Chesterfields between his knuckles, just right. Makes that smoke roll, outside his mouth, as he inhales the most natural breath a human can produce. He waves his hand to steer the plume away from me, if I am too close. Smoke is no good for me, only for him because he is grown. The man enjoys his cigarettes, like you're supposed to. He has a pedestal ashtray; the cupboard has books of matches with Pep boys and Camels on them. We have wooden matches, which I love, those pieces of splintery wood, with that beautiful topping of red and white that are magnificent. Mom smoked L&M, an all white filtered type. This was around the time when Kent "with the micronite filters" came out. Asbestos filtering added some modern sophistication. Most men would not touch a filter; the popular brands reminded me of the firecracker names. Pall Mall, Camels, Lucky Strikes for the Butts and for the 'works', Crab, or Anchor. Our milk gets delivered along with cake from the Dugan's truck. My knowledge of the world is miniscule. My family is perfect and if you don't say the same, we fight. None of the problems of yesterday, apply this afternoon. Rickey has three Lucky's. His Dad will never miss them; my friends are really good at taking things from their houses. This is a talent that I admire, and cannot understand, for good reasons. Universal Violence is the rule for my friends; they did not invent it. All of them are locked in a cycle of crime and punishment with their parents. How this system persists is beyond me? I fear my Dad and have almost never been touched by him as discipline. My Mom has an assortment of ineffective striking techniques. She really has no heart for the hitting, and claims it hurts her more than me. The dishrag is about her fiercest weapon. Unlike my Aunt upstairs who can really pick some cudgels. Her vacuum cord is a unique one, I respect it. This makes me seem much worse than my reality, which found a decent child in a loving household. One who wanted to smoke with Rickey, but was powerfully afraid of the consequences. Good thing Rickey had a plan.

In those times, in the Richmond Hill Community of NYC, not every property had been developed. Many were in that process as I grew up on 110th street, and created excellent places to play, hide, climb, and generally trespass. Looking back, things were enormously relaxed. A child or an adult, for that matter, was free to kill themselves in many ways that we aren't privy to today. My roaming almost always found openings where common sense should have barred access. My suspicions about the 110th street boys were that they had no self control; this proved somewhat true as time went by. What did that matter? They fulfilled the basic requirement for the "Safe Travel Manual": Always keep someone way out in front of you on virtually every expedition, which is the most crucial advice anyone can receive. Today was no different, mostly. The risk was on Rickey, except, All we had left to do was 'get a light'. Rickey's Dad used a lighter; something about that seemed sissy to me, but for sure, Rickey couldn't get the matches. Our plan was to go all the way up, past the Guilly house to the Construction, and climb the Concrete forms to get into the Basement Layout. Nothing down there but Framing, and no view from anywhere.

My only job was to get the matches, " just get them, Mike." This was something scary but do-able, and an entire book of Matches with the LSMFT on the back was in my pocket when we went North past 91st Avenue. Rickey was coaching me on the 'how to aspect' of the smoking, which was stupid. How could anyone not know how to smoke ? I was a little worried about the crew at the Construction, but not about smoking. That was something everybody had to do, like kissing girls. He did have a lot more experience than me on the butt science, having an older brother to ruin him. On the girl kissing, I was in the lead, two to nothing. On the cigs, Rickey had me, seven to nothing. I felt like a child in his presence.

When we started climbing the front steps of the 'Not a House', some people were passing by on the sidewalk. We just kept walking up, as if we lived there; actually it made us laugh to take the last step and vault onto the framing. All ready for the concrete pour, the upper surfaces of the structure were uneasy climbing. We jumped to the concrete slab below almost immediately. The jump was harsh, but you could not risk falling at this point of prep for concrete. Lots of rebar, or wire, or unfinished wooden edges, made a strong leap of about eight feet, a lot less risky than catwalking the top. You might break something while jumping too, but we had to be safe, didn't we ?

Time was a wastin', and we were hell bent to smoke all our cigarettes before emerging. This became a 110th street tradition. ALL the cigarettes had to be smoked before reentering the block. My book of matches was ready; cigarette number one was all mine. Rickey had good skills with the Match cupping, and a nice flame hit the end of that Lucky, as I drew a deep, sucking inhale of my first - aaaach kah naa, and I threw it down, as I retched and strangled. Rickey was punching my arm and back, too. Stepping on the butt was too much for him to take; my disgrace was complete. The thing had attacked me; it was obviously defective, or something. I knew smoking. This couldn't be smoking. Having my best friend from Kindergarden through third grade hit me did not even bother me.   "Geez, Rickey, why didn't you , TELL me ? " He couldn't laugh, he was too upset about the cigarette. Give him credit for being 110 street, all the way. As I climbed out, up the plumbing pipe, the only way out without a ladder, he was finishing the third butt. I had the thought that the Lucky brand was probably the problem.   " Yeah, Ricky, that's not my Brand." Good thing I was already back on the steps or Rickey would have given me the Headlock, for sure.

   This was another time that the run home was filled with emotions, the child that walked up the block was not exactly, the one who returned.

Chapter Eleven: Boys Clubber

The Boys Club, First Members, 1959, I am Number 27

  They are going to open a Boys Club on Atlantic Avenue, right on my block, just across that divided, major road.

  Here, in Queens, New York, Richmond Hill kids play on the street. My street, 110th Street, has lots of kids, and places to play. The tree-lined sidewalks have lines for box ball, except not the slates. Those blue slate walkways look nice. but they are no good for ball playing, though great for chalk drawing. The front steps of the houses have points for stoop ball, the traffic is light enough to allow chalk drawn board games, like Potsy and Hopscotch. We have Stickball bases and Skelly drawn, along with the 'Circle of War' divided like a pie. A game where you declare war on a country, presently repped by a player.   Everyone wanted USA, or their homeland: Italy or Germany, Poland or Ireland, forget Russia and Turkey. Japan was at war constantly in this game; we hated them, even more than Russia. You smash a ball down onto the piece of the War Pie and run away. If the Spauldeen was in use that country would be chasing a LONG way, before pegging any other nation. We had a game called territory played with knives, if you remember that far back. There was no lack of fun games to play.

  Even with the fun we were having, the thought of getting into that mysterious clubhouse as members was intoxicating. Rumors had it marked as a Socialist / Communist/ Secret House of Things we were to fear. How such a place went out of business, lost popularity, really is a mystery. My begging to join commenced, immediately; the activities listed were so phenomenal as to be dizzying. Hard to figure what my parents thought about it; they let me become a member right after school began in September. Miss Anne signed me up; George seemed to be in charge of the place. He was the full size, gym guy of the day, exactly three times as big as me, weighing approximately 250 pounds of upper body muscle, and wearing the sweat pants, tee shirt--WhistleCraft Clothes.

  The only other person worth mentioning was Cecil the Janitor, an immense fellow who spoke slowly, with the deep voice of the South. These were good guys; the sort that you would want running your place. And the CLUB was all that and more, man, what great activities!. Dozens of Pool Tables, real Tables, Bumper Pool, lots of cues. More slates and chalk. The upstairs gym was a full court, Basketball size , and a room full of mats to the left. Each of these rooms had an equipment room, full of the things needed for ALL the sports you could imagine and some, I never did.

Wrestling, Boxing, Tennis, Whiffle ball, Dodgeball, a kid might not do the same thing twice for weeks. The whiffleball games in that space were tremendous. The gymnastics were popular, too, with people tumbling heedlessly into others, and cartwheeling, pommel horsing, headstanding. The 'bloody nose room', I called it; I wrestled with friends there, and always lost. Seems there is more to wrestling than headlocks. I shot a lot of Pool, and improved as I learned more from some older guys. There were not a lot of members of any particular age; the whole place had 27 members when number 27, became ME. I could well go on about these great activities, but my main attraction to the club was the Bowling Alley. Yes, there was a total of five lanes: four lanes as you entered, then a walkway, then one by the far wall. Regulation lanes, where we set up the pins , down in the pits. We had Candle sticks and Duck pins, too. This type of bowling had a smaller hand held ball, without finger holes. Plenty of regular Bowling Balls were left behind by the mysterious ancestors who had been dispossessed. They may well have been alien giants, judging by the assortment of fingerholes.

There was usually an adult monitor in this area, sometimes that would be Miss Anne or maybe Bill V, a tiny athletic fellow, not much older than the members. During those times, we behaved like children. This type of behavior was the standard; members had respect in the club. Bad guys suspended their crappy attitudes here; it was THAT good. You had opportunity here, that impressed you down deep. Really, the place was too good for us. Occasionally, the room was left with what I would call Trustee Members. This was what I call, 'A Mistake' ! The instant the crew realized that there was unrestricted bowling the pieces would fly throught he air. Setting pins was never safe and if you were down range during Trustee Time, the risk was tremendous. Pins would be crashing up from the impact of full size balls and the duck pin balls might reach you on one bounce. Apparently, Bowling Alleys were indestructible and we were, too. The poor kids who were in charge tried to keep order, but it was hopeless.

This was a good example of how I became so very addicted to The Club. Within weeks of joining, every moment and thought, was wrapped up in the place. I ran there for each session, each day, twice on weekends. Life was perfect, my mind and body were completely occupied. Yes, completely, no block, no home, no schoolwork. I helped set up for activities, I dust mopped the gym; I helped Cecil with the Ash Cans. Three O'Clock found me, already at the front doors. Obsessed, I was, by the Boys club and it's people, new and different, from other schools and parishes, other ages and intelligence.

The "Johnnies" alone, were an infinite study. The ability to adapt to others was enlivened, like a challenge to my mind. No amount of words could say how much, I belonged to the Boys Club.

By the first School marking period, this impacted the report card. Open school night brought disaster. The adults, had it figured and figured right; I got banned from the Club. Banned and the Club knew it, too. Life was over; my marks immediately improved. My misery overtook my senses, school became the problem, nothing more than a game, of no value. Just a token to pay my entrance to the real world. Fifth Grade, Watershed of Bitterness.

I did eventually regain my privileges. Things weren't the same, though. This incident occured at a time when my education was being accomplished anywhere but at my little Catholic School. They'd given us the typical battery of tests at the end of fourth grade and made the mistake of letting me know my levels. Never tell a boy he is advanced; nothing good can come of it. Perhaps there should have been some special lessons, or even curriculum; there was not. The repetitive nature of regular classes became deadly boring, as the Sisters tried to remediate those in need, while steadily turning away from troublesome boys like me. That's the way I felt, and there was a lot of evidence that many false pretenses were being upheld. The world was revealing so much to me, and my mind was turning against one conformity after another. Soon after, I quit going to Church, at least I had friends to help me with that. There were still a couple of sheltered years of grammar school and they were peaceful. Sadly, my education stalled, then stopped. Each place I looked I found some tainted rust coating; the Club was one last moment of senseless commitment to fun. My time there was over, but so many followed and enjoyed the same, or even better experiences. The place is still doing the same great work, right now. Even better maybe.

Chapter Twelve: Hockey Skates

The Hockey Skates

Forest Park, The Frozen Jackson Pond, NYC, the winter home of Ice. Those Skates,

Oh, I got them for my Birthday, just a couple days before Christmas; they were the exact, iconic, Hockey Skates of the Big Timers. Brown, black strapped, big laces, rock hard steel-tips for the toes, shining silver steel blades. Crunching your feet much more than being snuggly, so tight and constricting that they hurt your chilly feet when you changed into them on the benches, next to the pond. The Thick White Laces would be tied together for carrying to allow the skates to hang over your shoulder on the walk. This was supposed to ease the load; it actually had the weight digging at your neck and the clunking boots batting your chest, but you looked cool as hell. To say that I loved my skates would feel so weak. I often spent time since my birthday, examining the edges of the blades, both sharp and flattened. They were not like figure skates, NOT. Men in figure skates were either too poor to have Hockies or, ?; it was 1961.

The super cold days of early December had the concrete pond at Forest Park frozen solid. The Ice breaker kids could not make more than a fishing hole before the freeze overtook it. Lots of classmates from my local Catholic school were spending their first of many winters at the Park. The Pond was big enough to give ample room to Older and Younger groups; the cold seemed to bring a peaceful commerce between all the Ice folks. Grown ups and tiny toddllers flopped together; the level was never consistently above crash cart. Circling was High style, and only a few Princess Ice Queen Ladies even attempted the Center Spinneroo. The ice, itself, always had unlimited ruts and limbs and leaves stuck in it. Jackson Pond would be a mix of very thin ice at one end, usually broken and unskatable. This area only held an inch or two of water on the western slope. From that tree-lined area heading east, the water got deeper and the ice much thicker. The last 150 feet of the pond became two or three feet of water covered by almost a foot of solid Ice. This expanse spread to about 100 feet wide, where the Pond area opened out toward the Apartment Buildings on the Catty Corners of Myrtle Avenue and Park Lane South. Myrtle Avenue, the southern border roadway, rose all along the south side fencing and the Hills of Forest Park did the same rise, on the parellel Northern side. The wind could only enter from the Southeast and that was always the kindest direction. The hawk from the North, would chase you right off the Ice.

Today was Christmas Eve, maybe the most bestest day a child could ever have. I was looking forward to seeing the girls from school and showing off my Manly Skates. A friend from school asked me to call for him on the way. He had not been up the park alone, and his Mom seemed to trust more in him, if he had a friend along. The kid was OK, just needed a boost. A bunch of Moms thought I was the ideal childhood buddy. My parental guidance was high level. They mostly liked my innocent look, which I played up. This was not even unusual, for my friend to be hearing the "be like Michael" garbage. I had been smoking for three years and just started drinking; I practised cursing and spitting. My marks were still 90's. Steven's Mom met us at his door, virtually shoving him out. We headed straight up the hilly last block to Jackson Pond.

Everything about the day was exciting, I loved being 'up the park', and acting any way I wanted, with people I hardly knew. The group of Skaters and Breakers today, are almost all friends, just different groups. The girls from my school are here, and that was very fascinating. They were so perfectly good and pure enough to make them insanely desirable, to me. Everything about my idea of attraction was wrapped up in these Catholic girls. If they ever had a thought of me, or gave me any attention, I would have run to confession. Why were they so grown up, while I was so childish? Women know everything, at least. My skating would let me show off, for these friends. The guys from school and the neighborhood were all around the place, some skating while others chipped at the Ice. Some of these local guys were 'Public' meaning they went to the Public Schools. Though friends of mine went there, the places had an awful stigma among the Catholic Schoolers. We had some tough guys in Holy Child, but my experience with the boys from P.S. 90 told me it was another realm of opportunity for mayhem. There was plenty about the world that I didn't know. I'd spent enough time with the Ice Breakers to know they would 'Be Skating' if the Money for Skates was anywhere near them. Getting out and about, opened the view into the lives of friends with DISadvantages. These might include a Dad, or exclude one; they could include problems, real or imagined. Frighteningly, some troubles were impossible to tell; and only shared with others by means of actions to interpret. Some of the boys and girls at the Park communicated with me, in that way. Simple signs of real deep stuff which touched me. My friends, included the Good, The Maybe Good, and The Good Grief.

Skating went great, time flew. Christmas Eve Perfection, except my friend, Louie Aquavelva, wanted to try my skates. "Can I hold your skates, hey, Mike"; "Five minutes, Mike"; "Please, Mike, I gave you those Cigarettes !" 1- NO, 2- NO, 3- No, 4- "After I 'm done, I will let you try, Louie." Nobody would stay that long; it was freezing, getting dark. Louie sat and stared; he had a sad puppy look that would not fool anybody. If Louie decided to take something, he would try. Fighting with Louie at the end of the day, no way I wanted that. We were friends. I wanted to go home. He had nothing in his life. My skates were only two days old; he waited, frozen in place on the bench. Worst of all, I had to remove my skates to walk home. OFF, they would have to BE. I was super torn, and decided to let him try, having made up my mind to throw down with Louie, one way or the other. Man, it was almost dark, seeming so late, when I handed my skates over. Thanking me a ridiculous amount, he laced them up, his feet bigger than mine, obviously. Offering to keep them until tomorrow, he began topple falling, slippetty skid falling, and making zero progress forward. We were using about five square feet of Ice; the place was almost deserted. Only the Ice Breakers, and the early Southern Comfort crew was left.

My Mom was cooking dinner and I was desperate. My feelings of anxiety were giving me fits. Begging Louie to finish, he said he would buy Hot Chocalate for me. Refusing any bribes, I insisted. Things were at a Point. I considered attacking him while he was on the Skates, but the plan had flaws. Eventually, over to the bench we went, off came the Skates and back in my hands. Louie wanted to buy that Chocalate; he was very joyful about his Skate, which would have sent many to the Emergency room. "Louie, I gotta' run" and man that was true. He literally hugged me and he was choking on the words, "Merry Christmas, Mike," "Merry Christmas."

You sometimes know, that you did the right thing. My thoughts turned to getting home, and the darkness that had now enveloped us. Laces over my shoulders, I ran. Down hill, toward Jamaica Avenue, so far and fast, I ran. My house could not appear soon enough, I was 'Late for Christmas Eve Dinner'. My Mom was cooking, I was so late. The skates pretty much battered me into submission before my feet slogged up my steps, near Atlantic Avenue. Knocking and Ringing, I prepared to be yelled at, and punished. How, Oh how, could I be such a moron on Christmas Eve?

My Dad opened the door, he told me, "You better get in here, Mike, dinner is almost ready."

I felt a Christmas Joy, the clock said 5: 30. Hugging my Mom made her say, "Michael, wash up for dinner, it's Christmas Eve" I know, Mom, I know.

Merry Christmas from me and Louie Aquavelva.

Chapter Thirteen: Rescue 8

Rescue 8

One of the original street action shows, when I was young, was about a rescue unit . Way out west, they were sort of Firemen/Medics. They, the two lead actors, got into all manner of super risky situations. Hanging precariously, jumping through flames or in the path of falling boulders, they almost got hurt daily, unless they actually got hurt. The injuries would make them look even more heroic, and they'd be quickly patched up, probably by the female sidekick 'Rescue 8' teammate.

The kids on my block loved the show and we had a club called Rescue 8, that met at a place we called Rescue 8. The place was the bridge and the Long Island Railroad tracks, near Victory Field. The centerpiece of the Cliff and Cavern type terrain was, "The Erosion."

The area just to the west, between Woodhaven Boulevard and the Rail Road bridge, had been pilfered by a developer. Spanking new Apartment Buildings now sat where once was a lake, wetland and Park. Now, as storm water cascaded from the bridge, it would rip around to the west end, and into the slope, headed south. The street drains could no way contain it, and the Quick turn and fall from the street was like rapids from the show, carrying some poor innocent "headed to the track bed below." This produced "The Erosion", a terrific gash of ten feet across, and eight feet deep. The sides were still unaffected at the top. The steeply etched banks were tortured and exposed to the elements. Dried roots and hardened dirt. The center of the pit, nothing but rocks.

As all children know, clubs must have initiations. That's a rule. The Rescue 8 club had one, and it was freakin' dangerous, to the point where the sidekick was not going to fix you up, if you bit it.

Part One - Walk the length of the bridge on top of the protective, outer concrete rail, and jump to the tree. The rail was about a foot wide, the drop on your right about thirty feet. The tree, only a tiny leap, to branches of two inches, at that height. Then, climb down.

Part Two - Climb the Metal Railway Tower and touch the Light Face Panel. The Climbing was Easy, but we feared the Wires, they carried RR Electricity.

Part Three - Run the Rescue 8, Obstacle Course. From the bridge, down the slope, through the gully of the erosion, past the tracks, around to your left, and up the gravel RR grading bevel, to the Crest of the erosion, in 60 seconds. Yes, we had a stolen watch.

You are Now Ready to BE, "Rescue 8' ed".

The Entire Membership stands on the far side of the gap, ready to catch you when you attempt the impossible leap across. Each one has tried and failed. Some came mighty close and were scooped up , "Rescued", as their feet and knees slammed into the face, after their jump.

More often, only the head and chest make it. The torso slams the bank, hitting roots, and rocks. Everyone will catch you. Everyone is, Ready to catch you. Backup, Run, JUMP. Welcome to the Club.

Chapter Fourteen: The House

Summer 1961, 110 St. Everyday, for the Eleven year old Mike.

Come on now, this is a regular place! There isn't anything unusual about my block. The children come out and play, everyday. They are so very nice and innocent. Why are some things so damn wrong ? Do other places have a "house" like this one, do they have a " family" like our cursed one here ?

These new "House" grown ups have children; they come out, sometimes. Not all the time. Thankfully, not everyday, but when these children come out to play... They are, Georgie and Henry, brothers who have a pair of the most sickenly, twisted minds you ever want to encounter. The smaller one is an absolute eel of slithering trouble; the older exists to plague others, and beat upon the head of his ranting little brother. Why both of these 'things' are so diminished and aberrant, is just plain blamed on their "house". The place is a nest for new arrivals, always full of problems, and soon to be departing for another tragic landing. Why they go, I do not know, but none have been missed. I am only eleven.

I am not a big guy, but bigger than Georgie, by a lot. Henry is my age, and my size, and just a scary proposition. For a year, the "house " has been exhaling these nauseating sibs. The time has been a test of the Good/Bad, inside all the kids, perhaps the worst for the Leftwich girls, who live next door to "it". While our days are full of nice games, we always make time to Glorify the evil of the "house curse".

Whenever, Georgie and Henry are allowed out, or escape their keepers, things follow a pattern with little change, only minor details differ. They are initially, disinterested in us, then they seem to notice us, The Us, who are either trying to act natural, like whistling and looking the other way, as if, a bear is walking down the street and we just have not noticed. Or we are literally preparing to buffer and batter these gruesome goons. They have always been the same, and our tiny society has accepted the grief they bring.

As, G and H, begin their socializing, the first salvo will usually be an inappropriate remark directed at the girls, or the smallest of the boys. At one time, these may have been jokes they heard. Now, they are nothing but insults being misused. An example might be, "Your hair looks like Rapunzel is a crazy nut", followed by expectant laughter. This giggling would contain the hope of some acceptance, as these were children seeking exactly that. Of course, after numerous previous, hideous outcomes, the maniacal Georgie was already becoming angry. Henry might be having a better day, as he had in the past. He was close to being a child, somewhat. Perhaps, like a broken toy. I always felt sorry for both of them and more so, their Mother.

Rejection from any child these boys encountered was assured, only the form changed. Lots of running away, some drifting and insulting, plenty of going back home with " My mom is calling me" excuses to flee. And of course, violence, which was never a good choice. When the fighting occurred, the sequence was this. Our villians would persist with their aggravating behavior, until one of the boys would punch them or kick them. Sometimes the girls would pop a few shots, whatever, then the screaming and crying.

The whole thing was horrible and pretty violent. The Geogie and Henry escapades were not funny. Even with little kids of sound minds, fighting is dangerous. Though I probably was more scared than anybody around, I often was the front man because of the Leftwich girls. They had to be defended from this awful creepiness, and harassment. This exact scene played out a dozen times, followed by the second most frightening part, "Mother House" emerging, and yelling, and swingng. This would rapidly bring Henry to his senses, as it instantly made Georgie into a rampaging animal.

Whatever nastiness had occured prior, was now piddling kid stuff. "Momma House", would try to drag the crazed Georgie inside, while Henry pummeled him. This did not seem to phase the "Housers", but the amount of revulsion and horror I felt was major. As I said, this was a routine on 110 St, but I guess I am sensitive, because I never had anything but fear of the whole thing.

Upon completion of her recovery mission, "Mother House" would come back out to lecture us on Christian fellowship. She smelled funny.

And now, the most horribly, horrid part, "Daddy House" comes home, enters, begins his blessings upon the "Housers". There is no one who can ignore it, as it is LOUD ! No chance to misinterpret these noises. My little friends and I sit flinching, on the Leftwich steps.

The summer of Georgie and Henry slips on by. The "House" is safe to walk by in the coldest parts of the winter. In the Spring, Georgie and Henry are gone, and the House has new Housers.

""THE PAFFELLINGERS"". Oh, do other places have a "HOUSE" ?

Chapter Fifteen: Tanzy Goes Crabbin'

Crabbin', at the Barges, North Channel Docks, Rockaway, New York

Summer of 1964, High School Freshman Mike, and the 110 Street Boys.

We got our Crab Traps ready; building them is a terrific little project. The flat cage sides, attached to the bottom square, put together at their base with metal rings and wire, so that the box trap opens, on all four sides when it hits bottom. Each side has a pull rope, of equal length, those four join, above the cage. When you pull fast on the Main Rope, the sides slap shut.

The bottom cage piece has a single wire, for stringing bait. We use Killies, or the best bait, Chicken. Crabs love Chicken. When the traps are rigged right, all you need is some weight to sink them, fast and straight. Of course, somebody has gotten' the clothes line ropes. Catching Blue Claw crabs is a full day outing for us, coming from Richmond Hill. The train takes forever to bumble south to the Rockaway Peninsula. The famous 'A' train now arisen from the Subway tunnels of Brooklyn, and crossing Jamaica Bay, Howard Beach, Broad Channel, and wetlands. This train line goes all the way to the Bronx, Northbound; that must take a week. We could take the bus down Crossbay Boulevard to the first bridge; they let you fish from that. The reason we are making the long trip is 'The Barges'.

Describing these behemoth, floating, metal slugs, is easy. They are floating soap dishes, that weigh about a million pounds a piece. Next to a barge, you are like the stem of a leaf. The movement of these jumbo critters was solely produced by the relationship between Jamaica Bay and the Concrete Piers. This created a slow, ever so slow, shifting and meeting of the Barges, the Piers, and The Tires. The tires were the "Thing". Cobbled on to the End Bumpers of each Barge were Immense tires, like tractor type sizes. The rubber was gnarled; the treads, mostly gone, but the width was still there. Between the Heavy Rope and the Tires, a barge had a bumper, about four feet thick, and eight feet high. This prevented the waters from smashing the beveled ends together, metal to metal. The movement would now crush the bumpers ever so slowly, instead. The power behind this crushing would be revealed by the noise from the rubber. The initial squishing, that you might expect, would be followed by squeals, pops, weeping, and grunts. These occurred as the gap was reduced to about four feet, total. Half the original distance. Here there would be a pause, a suspension of sideways motion, and a perceptible rising. We would have jumped on, as this began.

Our Crab lines went down the gap. Below were some pilings, and about thirty feet of black water. Jamaica Bay was awful polluted, then. The Dumps were open; people poured everything down the drain. There was no regulation of anything, made obvious by the way we roamed the Barges. Jumping around on the top of our waterworld tubs was dangerous. The gap was super dangerous; that is why we talked so much about Climbing the Tires. This stunt ranged from a common climb, to one completely unattemptable, depending on the Bay. At times, we could hardly stand on the Barges, due to the chop, or the Tide. Other times, the Barges would open a four foot gap, for a full minute. We climbed everything else we encountered, so why not this ?

Occasionally, the pilings below would snag a trap, we had lost a couple that way. We could see, it was possilble to climb the tires to a level below the crush; that was the place where Tanzy's trap got stuck. He wanted it, bad. His little brother was crying for his trap. This was like his 'Christmas Crab Trap', or some such, baby crap. Oh, Tanzy.

The day was a thirty-second-gap day; we were bouncing about a bit, up top, and not much of a tire-climbing-conditions day. The trap was well below the bumper line, Tanzy was sure he could reach that level in no time, get right back up, Tanzy was quick. I begged him to forget it; I didn't like his little brother, anyway. The gap began to open, rghasmhnfo, pop. Like a spider, Tanzy dropped onto the biggest tire, down ten feet. Only a reach to his right, and the trap could be jangled free. He was well below anywhere we usually crept, and the slime on the pilings and tires was much heavier. He looked up at me, with fear all over his face; he was not going to make it up in time. The gap was closing , in a way that seemed purposeful. The noises, rhhtne emmbopopossua, I was yelling, but I couldn't hear my friend's voice. The terminal rise came, with a slushy grunt.

That same opening sequence of noises and movements began, and brought a peek of Tanzy, his face half smeared with the slime from the pilings, half with red hysteria. Like a shot, he arose from his captivity, recapturing his nerve. He went to little brother, who was now crying. for real.

For a short time, they cried, together.

Chapter Sixteen: The Idjits

The Idjits, 1963

On my way to The High School Yard, to play Basketball. I have my new Cons' on, and tube socks; it's hot all this week in August, and today, Saturday, is no different. I can't help worrying that the Idjits will show up. There is no schedule for them; they appear and disperse. There are four of them. They may show up individually, or as a human wave of Idjits. Hey, Look, that is their name! I feel bad calling them by the name, but, by God, it fits the Idjits.

They came here from Stanslavakia, which I never heard of either. They are here, because of WW II. This makes no sense, like everything about them. Nothing about them is credible. They cannot speak English, and they never stop talking. Their clothes are so close to the ones everyone wears, yet, on the Idjits, they resemble costumes. No two of them, clothes or people, have any similarity to the others. Almost magically unique, these boys are, at best irrepressible. At worst, they are an invasive species. No matter your age, they have that. Any sport you play, one is on your team. Whatever you do, there is your own, personal Idjit.

No one likes the Idjits, but they are hard to hate. They think friendliness is like the air. They like everybody, all the time. They cannot understand sport; they are likely to kick the Basketball, or punch the Football. Sometimes I go to another park, because of their nonsense. No amount of shunning has any effect . Our bully, Krugell, has hit each and every Idjit. Multiple times. They don't even get angry. I swear, I don't like them. At all. They are amusing as hell, though. If you think about them, you just laugh. I wasn't good at hating when I was young. They were a nuisance, but that never discouraged them at all. Wherever they came from, it must have been one horrible place.

Today is almost perfect. My Basketball game is scuffing up my cons' nice. Everyone stepped on them, as soon as I got here. The Idjits are late. Three o'clock comes and goes. We finish our last half court game before the boys show up. They are not right, they don't intrude, even in the conversations. So different is their behavior, that we ask them, "What's up, Idjits ?"

I'm pretty sure we cannot really understand what they are telling us, because it draws us in, closer and closer. The Idjits are getting, De sPorted, depro torted, what,

what ? We are all American boys, Idjits or not. Just because you're an Idjit, from Stanslavakia, that's no reason to get kicked out !

   The boys are sad, downhearted, broken, hopeless, and rightly so. Their heavenly stay here is over. All the sweet fun, for them, is done. Only now, do we realise our place in the world for the first time. I fully see why the Idjits dove, head first, into everything. This made me think, so hard. My cons' were still Perfect. I looked at Isaac Idjits' miserable skips. I tried to look away, but too late, too damn late. When we swapped, I tried real hard to laugh, which sounds like a choke, I guess. Anyway, it was a long time ago, and I don't believe Stanslavakia is real, anyway, anyway.

Chapter Seventeen: Twin Lakes

The camera is above us and circling, like a drone view of our little expedition. Mr. Revins, his son Harry, and the seven of us, waiting on the bus stop outside of Westfall's Restaurant and Bar on Atlantic Avenue and 111th Street. Waiting for the Q 37 bus to take us to Queens Boulevard.

The wide expanses of these roads lets the camera swoop in, from the North and reveals the faces of some happy boys. The oldest is 13, the youngest 10. Mr. Revins is a really old guy, in a vest, on a summer day. He is dressed more like an office manager, than someone taking his son and seven little friends fishing. The camera zooms in on the flask in the vest's inner pocket. His gray whiskers complete the W.C Fields profile.

The view, down 111 th Street, has the bus, the Green Bus Line, pulling out of the 95th Avenue stop, and heading for us. Mr. Revins shouts, "Get those coins ready, boys. I ain't paying for any of you." The cost, fifteen cents. My Mom said it was OK, long as I stayed near the Tanzy brothers. She didn't trust Harry's Dad to watch us; she just knew the Tanzy's could hold down the fort, in any situation. Their Mom was her best friend. We scuttled up the steps and onto the bus, dropping our dime and nickel, clanking and snagging our poles and hooks, under the searing hot gaze of the Driver, in his Official Hat and wearing his Arm Badge. The coin box jingled, as he observed each coin throught the glass sides. Lord knows, the passengers were horrified, when I spun my way into the aisle, with my two piece, 12 foot Lunker Landing net. The camera pans down the length of these poles and onto a prim looking lady, grimacing. like she smells something foul. We run to the rear seats, soon as possible.

We can hear the chatter from inside the bus, as the camera follows above showing the slow crawl of the bus, through the winding Richmond Hill, Forest Park route of the Queens Boulevard run. The neighborhood is only half visible, due to the many tall trees lining every street. The only break is the Elevated train on Jamaica, snaking to the East and West . Before long, we have arrived. Last stop, right outside the Old Hospital, and on the South side of Queens Boulevard. Bumbling out the back doors of the bus, after waiting for all the real people to be let off first, we head into the Subway for our trick passage across the road. Queens Boulevard, is so wide that we always use the subway tunnel for crossing. The camera awaits us, in the corridor, next to the turnpike, where the wind and sound of the speeding traffic slap you. The walk under the road is so very dank, that our emergence into the sun blinds the camera for an instant. We stand at the highest point of our journey, now to the fun part.

From here, we begin descending to our Twin Lakes. From the super civilized world of Kew Gardens and Hospitals and High Rise Apartment Buildings, to the bottom lands of, soaked grounds, and weeds, reeds, moss, and wildlife. Quickly, and steadily downhill, we almost slide, to the bridge across the Grand Central Parkway. Concrete and steel still hold their sway on the land and the mind here, but our minds are already just around the bending stairway on the far side. Down those stairs, lined and insulated, by such dense greenery, and at the base of those steps, where the stream begins. There, the hold of City life is cracked, unwoven, forgotten.

The camera looks straight ahead, to the limited view, down the stream, from just above, the Stone walled Outlet, that initiates, and controls the headwaters. The sides or banks expand only slightly, to about six feet and the depth is less than knee high, but taking a lower angle it shows a frog, staring up at us. Turning back to our safari team, the camera shows faces of children, full of anticipation.

The stream offers two good choices on how to proceed. Expanding, as it runs, away from us here, the left side is only grassy path, the right bank, has an asphalt pathway. The NYC Parks Department is the Keeper here. As we split up for the first walk/stalk up the sides, the camera rises to reveal the entirety of the place we call Twin Lakes. The eyes must readjust to gather the new vista ahead: the stream, the wooden bridge; the first lake is still 200 yards away. The first lake opening to the north, and reaching away to the west, for a mile. There joining a second, larger lake thru a tiny, coupling inlet. The place is almost ten square miles of water, and wetlands. The place we call Twin Lakes is actually the site of the 1939 Worlds Fair, on the Western Border. We always enter from the East, through an undeveloped storm drainage path. This kind of represents us, in a way.

The camera swings back to my face, holding tightly to my now 12 foot turtle hunting net, sneaking westward. Then, down, almost right next to me, to a smiling turtle with colorful stripes. We love Twin Lakes.

Chapter Eighteen: One Ten Boys

April, 1962

Holy Child Jesus School, 7th grade. I have two sets of friends. School and Block, starting with the Boys Club and 110th street. Go everywhere I can, Forest Park, 106st Park, Richmond Hill H.S. schoolyard, and excursions to friends' blocks.

Walk home from school, the same way everyday, with the regular crew. The girls are friends, all of them, as far as I know. Can't picture how anyone doesn't think of me as a friend, but jealousy, competition, and goading can make boys into enemies.

My boys, on 110th street. are a hard bunch. They've taught me that life contains fights, period. There are few excuses accepted, and cleverness will not avoid all these matchups. By understanding my place in the violence pecking order, I've minimized my actual fights. No top dog, fight boy, beats on the same friend, repeatedly. Only crazy small fry challenge above their heads, excepting emotional outbursts. You do not wish to smash the weak, more than once in awhile.

Today, walking down 111th street, Gord, from 107th street wants trouble with me. The reasons are no interest to me; this punk is soon on his back saying, "I give up." Incredibly, no sooner do I accept his surrender, without punching and let him up, He wants more! The crowd, of boys and girls, is as shocked as I am.

Quickly, he is on his back, with my knees pinning his shoulders to the ground. He can struggle, but he will be on the ground, til I say So. You already know he will say, "I give up" and he does.

NO, no- I crack him, three in the face. He cries hard. My shots were merciless, 110 style. I let him up. He is done. The boys are mad at Gord; the girls are mad, at ME !! never knowing I could be so mean. HA, that's funny.

Now, I'm done, it's over but . . . Wayne from 107, wants to fight me , too.

Really, it was him making Gord act so stupid. I never would have known what I can see now. The girls liked me, that was all it took for these boys to fill with hate. Anyway, as I just finished a fight and a half, I ask for a postponement, til 4 o'clock. In that childish landscape, such chivalry existed, on 107th street.

At, Four o'clock, by 110th street and Jamaica Avenue, by Mc Governs' Bar. Up my block, I went to my meeting, not real happy, and alone. Now for the best part.

On the way up to Jamaica, Ricky meets me. Even though he must know the deal, I do not want to ask for help. No need, Ricky is in ! We arrive; Gord and Wayne are there waiting. They definitely had me in mind. I have lost my taste for any of it. Not Ricky! He tosses Wayne around, while I stare at Gord. Old Waynie continues to tell me, how much he is gonna' kick my ass.

From me, just Laughs, and NO worries. Nobody from school will come near me again. I am from 110.

Chapter Nineteen: Trophy Time

Who Won?

I am in a world of summertime.   Ball all day and hang out all night. Well, til 11, anyway. Mostly very little to do, when being sixteen is not letting you have the regular money and transportation to much, besides sitting on steps at the High School telling the friends you just played a game with about the game.

Tomorrow, we will have a Handball Tournament, run by the director of the H.S. summer camp. We hang at the yard anyway, why not get in it? The level is low amateur at best. I also play at 106 park, where the best in the area compete. There, I am a little scrub. At the schoolyard, I might be the best.   Only a couple of the guys are any good at all. We do have a problem. though.

We have Krugell, yes, that one. He is two years over the 16 age limit and can play. He does all the time, and cheats and bullies his way to a lot of wins. Both me and my best friend. Johnny are better, which could get dangerous. Squealing on his age is out of the question. We all get to use the pool and gym during the summer, and ageing out Krugell would hurt him bad. As well as whoever did it.

So, we gotta mess with him for the Championship and the trophy which is pretty nice.

The semifinal between Johnny and myself is decided in a close game in front of a bunch of friends. I win the right to face the choice of what to do to our bully "friend". I should beat him in a fair game. I want to beat him, but I know how sore he is when losing. This is so bad a temper, it intimidates all the kids. We start the final game with a few spectators. I begin to cut and roll the ball high on the wall driving Krugell back and forcing errors. This volleying game is making him so angry that most of those watching, walk away, around the side of the building. They fear to even watch Krugell when he is this excited.

His strategy is wetting the ball with sweat and hitting hard so it skips or skids.

Losing all control of my wits, I continue slicing high shots to counter the power of my raging bull opponent. Tired but in control, I finish the job, while Krugell yells and threatens my existence.

At the last point, Exhausted, I just sat down against the wall. Not one person saw the finish. Man , that is respect for the bully!!!   Maybe Krugell had in mind to pummel me, I do not know. He walked around the building , where all the other kids were and I was happy to see the back of him.

When I got up and went around the corner my friends said congratulations as I walked to the directors desk inside. That trophy was real nice and I earned it, except. ..

Krugell had gone straight to the desk inside, lied to the director and took off with HIS trophy!!!

I tell you truly, that trophy was never seen again.

Chapter Twenty: Double Agent

November, 1966   Big 16

Basketball, as a Double Agent.

HCJ, Holy Child Jesus School, my past and part of my present. Everyone made me 'a good boy'. Already a boy without a hint of trouble, they worked extra catholic sternness, to insure any decent child knuckled under. They bred rebellion, among the thoughtful. How young do you have to be, to miss the mean spirit. Anyway, I played ball for the parish teams, even after graduating to High School.

The Tyro Basketball group had strict age limits; as a sixteen year old, you were too old. For tournament purposes, with organizations outside the catholic league, rules got fuzzy and plenty of "ringers" were added to rosters. Such an event was the Police Athletic League tournament of Queens County. Lucky ol' Mike, got added, not cause I was so good, just muscle. Mostly peaceful, travel teams in basketball do sometimes rumble a bit. Truly the cupcakes of sport ruffians, HCJ basketball players were all mouth, and practically zero violence. Amid this culture, my reputation as a thug was stone. Just one block away on Jamaica Ave, that would be laughable. My truly violent friends were not even major players in that rumbling world.

Sadly, incongruently, we managed to have some kind of fight, at every stop and each game. None of them amounted to more than barking spats; there were detectives hanging out. We came pretty close to getting hurt one night, when people threw weights off the track above the court.

All the games had been road trips, where you pile in some car and go. Parents, coaches, any ride, who cares how you get there? You might get some creepy peeks into family life on the trip. This is how we got to Hollis Hills, for this to unfold.

During the game, which was very good (and we lost to a team of guys with beards!) some of the little baby pricks on our bench mouthed off to the crowd. They, local boys, were young Asian kids not associated with the team. So very strangely, they were actually a gang Looking like children. These little guys were no joke and made it clear they would be attacking us, after the game. When I heard this crap later, and who was causing the problems, my head boiled. Our kids were there with daddy and were the punkiest, most useless boys around. Worse still, the team was so scared that they stayed in the locker room, until I had to yell at them. The adults on this trip

46

were strangely invisible, very possibly scared themselves. We had young kids along.
Only a few of the players had any heart. It was a situation.

  Before we walked out of the gym into the night, I told the few with me to stay tight
and SHUT up. If you can do that alone, it makes all the difference between nothing
happening, and incoherent chaos. We got to the vestibule, met the opposition and
were cursed and threatened.   It was nothing, I say worse to my friends. Stupidly, a
prideful guy on my team talks back! He, Gets called out, and starts to square off, as
soon as we exit. He lasts about ten seconds and runs inside, where I guess the rest of
the team is hiding. There are two of us, outside the door, and ten kids from Hollis,
more than ready to go: and they do!

  In a quick sequence, one runs at me, swings his right, too high and my left forearm
strikes it. He rebounds and yells, I hurt him bad. Another, gets thrown to my right,
into a terribly placed sticker bush; believe me , he howled. I notice my friend Greg ,
standing behind me and fighting and little Tony coming out of the door. Tony goes
down, almost immediately with three on him. Tony is getting a beating; but it gives
me and Greg the advantage on the rest, who can't mount an attack on us. These kids
are too small, and are living out a fantasy of violence.   Me and Greg manage to get
Tony inside, and regroup. The team is hiding in the locker room. I do go in, and
scream at them, tell all of them, "when we meet at the park, we are gonna, GO !"
A few adults have materialized and milled about. Myself, and a couple of adults, and
Greg , walk out.   The kids are gone, typical gang style.

  When this young man, who is both a tough guy, and a good boy, looks into the car
parked right in front, he sees The Punk who started this crap, in the car, WITH HIS
FATHER.

    There...the WHOLE time, sliming up my world!

Chapter Twenty-One: Porch Cats

My Front Porch from 1960, Always, up until 1975. People and Cats.

Here in Richmond Hill, NY, lots of homes are built with a front porch. Simply, a part of the Victorian style and the neighborhood life. Ours featured the classic deck, posts and fencing, doorway enclosure, and windows, all of wood. Richmond Hill is "stickbuilt", white posts, and rails, gray floors, and green trim. Sitting above the front, the six steps of our stoop, are facing east; this was a space for grown ups and kids, to visit, view the terrain, and just relax outside the house.

For our family, it was also the main place to see our cat. We always had one; he always stayed, outside, all summer, and lots of the winter. He was an animal. Untamed, unaltered, male as all hell. Dangerous, aggressive, well known and feared. Often despised, seldom befriended by our neighbors, our cat would do as it pleased, to anyone and everything, that allowed it.

Barring the threat of violence, these "Toms", would rule the world. They prowled the locale in search of victims and mates. Countless complaints were registered by the porch passersby.

Three different boys, filled the role of the "Schneider's Cat". The first was Cicero, a striped gray and black fellow. I grew up with him, for sure. He put a few bites and scratches on me; I learned how to handle ferocious animals from him. By the time I was ten, Cicero had flown from the porch, enough to get his attention. He was an awful bully, and I loved him, tremendously. As time went by, he began to lose more fights than he won. His head remained unbowed, but with chunks missing. He faded away in the late sixties, and I was old enough to be in charge of his departure. He was so massively naughty that the locals remarked about his absence and shared stories of the hideous pest. He had actually entered a few homes, stealing a whole chicken from one. My chest was bursting with pride.

He was replaced almost immediately, with Whizzer, an all white demon of a Tom. The cat began striving for turf, with everybody and everything, before he was two pounds. Our relationship never did get completely past violence. He would challenge me and cause some nasty damage. That cat could fly. I launched his ass, a few times. We mostly got along, or some moderate threats would back him up. He did not accept any master, ever, and continued the Cicero tradition of jumping up on people's laps, to be petted, feared, or whatever these cats thought you should do about it. Most of our seated guests endured these staring contests without incident, petting, or movement !! This sometimes required my intervention and the cat would " give me the look". " Why are you doing this?", he would ask, "This is our porch"

We had to replace Whizzer eventually, his white head did not grow into the beautiful battle scarred noggin of Cicero. He looked as bad as he was. Fighting nightly got the best of him. Surely, he reaped the benefits, but sadly, the regrets as well. His successor was Smoky, and he brought his own dimension to the lap staredown. Smoky seemed to have an insanity, that truly frightened most. Explosive temper was his hallmark. As committed porch catters, we stuck with this boy. That was not easy, as he attacked people and other cats in broad daylight. He was a...cat sociopath. Only a smack sufficed, as he never acknowledged any threats. Had I thrown him the " just amount", he could have earned frequent flyer trips to see Mickey Mouse. I often had to ban him from the porch, altogether.

These cats and their way of life are long gone. I suppose that I look like an awful brute and I truly did clobber these animals, before they would knuckle under. They bring me to say the world has changed along with our relationship to our world. Today, animals live in preserves, captivity, or are altered to our liking. Civilized or Sterilized.

I did see a tiny, free, turtle this morning, and I let him GO.

Chapter Twenty-Two: Big Lew

Richmond Hill High School, Schoolyard. Freshman Mike, 1963

This big old High school is squeezed into the cubby of three city blocks, and the smack middle of one. If the design were to open up toward Avenues or Concourses, the various facades would look excellent.   Instead, the poor big duck sits in a pile of leaves. All the stately plumage covered by boring little houses that are too close.

The schoolyard has the best spot on the property. Facing north, behind the pool wing, it catches shade then sun, as the day goes by. For me, this place is the main feature of the school. Who cares about the classrooms and auditoriums?   I love the yard and the pool, especially the yard.

The area is defined by the dimensions of the rear of the school, and the triple decker fence to the east, north, and west. The divisions, formed by the wing for the pool, are perfect for a ball field, basketball court, and an alternate open space right beside the pool house extension. All of these are made, just for me. The group of kids who play here exist, just for me. I can enter by the 113th street gate, on the southern corner, play in the softball game there, or keep going to the right, and check if the pool is open. Mostly, I walk by both toward the basketball court. There might be a game of stick, or handball, around the corner to my right, as I pass the edge of the pool house.

Just about every day, I walk to the schoolyard. Thinking about myself and hoping to be stronger and taller and jump higher. Thinking about the dunks I will be throwing down, when my vertical leap increases, just two inches. Seems like I will be six, and not seven, feet tall like I planned.

Lew Alcindor is at Power Memorial H.S. One year ahead of me in school. Big Lew is almost a legend already ! They had a picture of him, with his fingers wrapped around the rim and his toes on the ground, in the Long Island Press. The world is changing, and Lew will do his part, a young black behemoth, the idol of NYC kids lke me, and a horror to older generations. Such a fright is Lew, that they change the rules when he enters College level basketball; No dunking anymore, Lew!

Horrid travesty of sportsmanship!   The emotions he must have felt! He was just dominant, his color scored no baskets. Rarely has sport so honored an individual, and disgraced itself, the only time I know of is, Wilt. They changed the basketball court's 'key' area to prevent his dominance. At the same time as this attitude existed at the high levels, the ground zero of race relations was poppin'. The courts were allowing real people to interact and actually overcome a little bit. Small steps they were, I am still walking along with others, away from this past.

At this time, my thoughts were always filled with fantasy accomplshments of the near future. Filled to the point of missing some real life opportunities. Gifted and strong, I mostly played basketball for fun, competed without commitment, dreaming of a physical dominance well beyond reality. Were I to have trained and applied myself, much like the activities in those classrooms I mentioned, I would have reached better levels. As it was, I never even tried out for my High School team, lacking the confidence to face that challenge. Convincing myself of my inadequacy and avoiding the rejection. Honestly, I didn't know how to play seriously, but that is what coaching could have done for me. I see later, that many young athletes have support and guidance. A person doing it on their own is pretty rare. I wonder when Lew got steered onto the courts.

Of course, at the same time you are thinking about sports, life is challenging you. You are finding High school life difficult, too. Not so much the new subjects, if you try. Ah, there lies the same problem. Being undercut and judged, by outer and inner forces. There is competition in the world outside, and doubt inside. Many is the word expressing the thought that, young people need to have confidence, oh MANY. Please envision a world where all the doubt is gone. Where competition is met with effort, challenge with enthusiasm. Not by some, not sometimes, but always and without rest. Brings to mind Bees, who are reported to do something like this. They don't. When observed, they were found to have some bee bums, laggards, unemployed bees.

When an ant colony was observed gathering, some of the ants let others do all the work! What kind of ant crap is that ?

Our High School Yard Colony had some ants doing their own thing. The place was my place to be great, and mediocre at the same time. Anyway, I loved that place. Had fun there and friends. Knew boys and girls who were about as perfect as myself. That was exactly how I liked it.

Chapter Twenty-Three: Madison's Day

Tackle Football, Winter of 1963

Good Jesus, it was so bitter cold up by Queens Boulevard. All of my teamates were whimpering about it before we even got off the Q37 Bus. The whole idea of running this rematch football game with the Chargers seemed like trouble anyway. Now the weather was turning toward disaster. After so much planning and preparation the game was going to go off, no matter.

Having no fields around our area to hold these rivalry games made them special, actually. Lugging ourselves and our gear up to Twin Lakes, in Flushing Meadow Park, involved a whole day of Team Unity. This was very important for the Vikings, my team. We had a little less of everything needed to be a traveling Football squad.

The Chargers had better Helmets, better pads, by far, and they had...Team Jerseys with Letters and Numbers, AND their Names !! Our stuff was like cheapo hand me down junk in comparison. They were a lot more Organizally, as well. We had a number of guys who had never followed an order in their lives. The contrast was obvious, and made for a sweet bitterness on our part. Our past games were always smashing successes. The Vikings main plays were simple runs , mostly right up the middle. This allowed Big Tommy Bam to carry the a ball and six or seven Chargers about ten times a game. The passing game was similar in sophistication, having me and other end go deep, over and over.

NYC Football, on our level was mimicking High School Programs. One of these locals' programs was at John Adams H.S. Some of their lineman had been playing with the Chargers in the last matchup. This really was unfair and we did complain. We had a few casualties resisting these clods and each one of us wanted revenge. In the spirit of good sportsmanship, we had recruited two of the running backs from the same program. One was a long tall speedster and the other was, Madison Day.

Madison Day was a muscle. On top was a head muscle, just below, without an interruption for any neck, stood the Largest Madison muscle, atop two legs of sinuous Day muscle. Why anyone would play against Madison Day is for the scholars to answer. He agreed to play for us because of the girls we bring everywhere. This part is easy to understand. His fellow running back, Tall Guy , is along for the ride, I guess. These two are SO intimidating that the Chargers threaten to quit, before we even start warming up. The field is a rock hard pan with frozen grass and bumps all over, caused by the ice underneath. Right next to the first lake, it is soggy all summer and wind swept sandpaper all winter. I am feeling my socks get crispy and the crappy helmet is freezing to my ears. I hesitate to remove it for fear my ears will come off too.

Strangely, our Captains have agreed to let Tall Guy play for the other team, as long as we get Madison Day. We line up without delay. The winter theory is "soon as we start playing the weather won't bother you at all"; this is crap today. The temp.is 15 F , and the wind off the lake is slicing you a new part in your frozen hair.

We receive the Kickoff. I sadly elect to field it on about the fouth skipping bounce. Running straight forward and colliding with players from both teams relieves my plight and we go on offense. The handling of the Football is very difficult, stalling plays and allowing defenders to easily smother them. Both Madison and Tall Guy score touchdowns on great individual runs. I score on a trick play that causes a long argument about the rules. The end result is: I do not score, and the Half ends six up { no kicks allowed}.

The day is getting short, as we kickoff the second half, the sky is darkening and the conditions are brutal in every way.   Your lips can stick to the face mask!!   The game is tense and tiring, and a few more casualties line the sides.   Madison Day is playing Safety on defense, behind my side cornerback. The Chargers have run our way a lot. The field gives me and Madison a big advantage in the first half, being virtually uphill for the runners, but now. . . The sweep is making progress on me. Tall guy is flying around my corner. My angle is good, the sideline is forcing him to turn back to me, slightly. We are both going fullout, to my right side.   As I pump my right hand running, it is brushed back to my body. Madison Day is passing my right, with speed and at a really low level, like a torpedo. Tall guy is playing me high with his elbow, when Madison Day Explodes through his right leg.

Tall Guy lays on the frozen, misshapen surface of lakeside with a broken leg.   Freezing and smashed, and trying to hold together, he looks such a wreck. Everything is just not worth a damn right now. We are ten minutes walking from any help, so alone in this empty field.

Madison Day picks his friend up in his arms and begins walking. He carries him all the way to Queens Boulevard, without a word between them. Madison Day and Tall guy. Never saw them again and,

I never played Tackle Football Again.

Chapter Twenty-Four: Graduation (precursor A)

June of 1967, Graduation Ceremony, Outdoors at JTK High.

Here I am walking the walk, throught the Commencement of our four years. The real action will be afterwards, back in our Home rooms where Diplomas and Certificates will be given out.

Due to late tests and Regents results, I don't know if I will be completely finished with this hideous chapter, at this clown fest. There are so many things wrong with this school, among the very worst is my attitude. I've made so much trouble for myself, needlessly, unless you consider that a young man must think. Thinking here, meant confronting a place of hodge podge rules made by rookie clergy and enforced by force. There are no traditions, the place is only five years old and we are the second graduating class. Everything was made up as we went along. The boys and girls are on separate sides of the building, only combined in the huge cafeteria at lunch. That is, if you call being kept divided in that room, combined. The idea of this sickness alone was troubling. The building itself was settling into the swampy cemetery where it was built. When you rode the bus to your stop, the roof of the school was below you, down in the hole, surrounded by graves and a Railway line. The cross on top only emphasized the plight of this poor misplaced goose. The steep hill to the entrance was not paved until my Junior year.

We were routinely pummeled in the sports arena, as late comers with no Senior class. The Catholic League was super strong, and I have to give a lot of credit to those guys and girls who tried valiantly to represent our Hole' school. There was a certain lack of spirit that was combatted by Pep rallies and announcements. The announcements were often made by a Brother, a sweet fellow, with a thick accent from his homeland. He would build enthusiasm, until his speech was using English in new ways. He once said, "You have to, need to, get to, want to, beat the Molloy, the crickets in the basement are message to me to get to need, to get, this beating." He was hilarious and there were a lot of good people at JTK, I was not one of them. I was an incorrigible problem child. immature and manish as hell. Defiant and flippant, reluctant to cooperate on principle, managing me must have been an awful chore. How I got this way, I don't want to say, but it was not any one thing. If it was, mostly one thing, it was my damn brain, which absorbed effects too well. My days were like a sensory overload; everything amazed me and I was part of the sixties, anyway,

I am at the Graduation and back at my Homeroom. Our teacher gives out envelopes that contain our actual fate, be that Diplomas, or notices about additional requirements, or failures. You might have to go to summer school or even repeat the grade. This could happen to some of my class, or me. I needed to have some tests results confirmed, to know the contents of my Envelope.

When I am handed mine, some of my classmates are razzing me pretty hard. My academic failures are well known; my repeating the whole grade is a worry for my friends and a hopeful joke for the others. Strangely, my envelope contains a note to report to the Office of the Dean, this is not right. Mr. Kully confirms the message; they want to see me. I am truly confused, the year is over, the results are in. If I have failed and need remedial work, there is no issue. There might be reason for the staff to feel disappointed, they did try hard to steer me right, but there is no reason for them to 'see' me! Saying, what is to be a final goodbye to my classmates, a few saying, "You will catch one last smack at the Office," I walk to my appointment with Doom.

Of course, I imagine some perfectly awful things as I stroll the long, long corridors of JTK toward the Dean's. When I enter Brother's Office, as I have many times before, the Principal is also there. This makes no sense at all, what ? They quickly inform me that I have passed just enough classes to receive my school Diploma. OK, I am overjoyed, but ?

Then, without modifiers, I am informed that I have also passed enough Regents Exams to receive my REGENTS Diploma, as well. Apparently, this has been such a shock to them that they now have honored me with this jaundiced tribute. As if to curse the outcome, I am not sure they even knew what was the point of the meeting. I had to ask permission to leave, as they had nothing else to say. I behaved very respectfully, as I thought they might come to their senses.

I know every young man wants to feel special and this was a real Honor. Yossarian !!

Chapter Twenty-Five: Precursor B

The New York City of Spring 1968,

I had a job, the sort of thing that was surrounded by time, and had little hope of survival.

E.F. Hutton, Brokerage, a real life, concrete location, way downtown. The same block as Trinity Church, about 156 Subway stops from my house in Queens. I am an order clerk, in a room full of order clerks. We handle a little rack full of Buy and Sell Slips. Columbus was still a good guy. My office was fifteen floors up. Battery Park was at the end of the block. The Mets were like a new toy without assembly instructions, but ready to insert Batteries.

The 'J' train took it's stumbling roll, through Brooklyn above ground. That is why we called it, the EL', short for elevated. Nobody in America had used the term Middle East. World War II was giving way to Viet Nam in minds across the country. We were avoiding the Domino Effect. People were fighting about segregation in the schools, on television, but on the J train every passenger could tell you the TYPE of neighborhoods we were above.

I went to work on a lot of days, most days I would say. My boss, Mr Stanley, seemed to think that Order Clerks should work every day. He got me the job, making my Mom very happy. As a young adult in 1968, my own ideas were froggy, prone to be green, centered mostly in the thigh area, and jumpy. The tendency was to sit very still, until startled into senseless action. Anyway, I had to call in hungover, quite a bit. My girlfriend was a bartender at the Big Bar, right beneath my train station. You can agree, I'm sure, that this required mr. schneider to spend most of his pay protecting his assets. She worked in a room full of Order Clerks, so to speak. Two or three days a week, I returned to work, almost directly from her place. This could not last and before long, I was fired from both of these positions. Interestingly, the two managers both told me, in tones filled with bile, "I have Changed my Mind !"

Now, I had played myself, into the impossibly perfect position all young men are aiming toward, Jobless, without prospects, desperate, and happy. I wanted nothing to do with any future, what so EVER. My daily routine of hanging out was suited to my needs. As long as I avoided any thinking, I was golden. Remember, we handled almost 15 million shares of stock on Wall street in those days. Big numbers had one comma. There was no WTC, the Dollar was worth ten Marks. The hitching across

Europe was a Thing. My hair could grow, and that was enough for me. Nothing was going to make me become an adult. Jamaica Avenue had Hippie stores selling used flannel shirts. There was Basketball to play and beers to drink.   I had five different crowds to bounce off.   I ask you, What could Go Wrong ?

Chapter Twenty-Six: Precursor C

America, 1969, Where everything was given to me.

It was a place, where youth was moving and deciding. Many were becoming aware of choices, pathways as new as themselves. Much was made of the freedom being gained, and the repressions, rejected. This story is about one, of very many, floating through this life, directionless and apathetic. Standing carelessly, at the bank of a swiftly moving stream, unable to act.

The consequences, obvious to a nineteen year old, are not sufficient to cure his bad attitude and apathy. So, he gets drafted into the U.S. Army. Physically fit and mentally unprepared, he endures training and receives orders to be sent to the 'Republic of Viet Nam'.

Even at this point, he is just carried along. A virtual stickboat, floating down a rain filled curb!

Upon his arrival, things rapidly challenge him, and end his childish ways.

Chapter Twenty-Seven: Morris, Norris & Horace

October 1969, Fort Jackson South Carolina

The Story of Morris, Norris , and Horace. I'm in it, too.

There are a lot of different sort of guys here in Basic Training. They come from all over, and sound like where they come from. I am from Noo Yawk so I speak a little fast and harsh. Norris is from Brooklyn, so we understand each other. Other people understand us, too, even if they don't know what the hell we are saying. This just isn't the case with Morris and Horace; they come from places that speak slow and deep and drawl, if you can call Panamanian a drawl. You had to listen hard, if you wanted to get their meanings.

We are cooped up in a barracks and next to each other, all day. That is plenty irritating, and   Norris is always angry; he practices at it. He told me that in his neighborhood a little flaw in your rage could be detected. He was a muscular, slight, very black cat, and very Cityfied, like me, except I am so white. I am not capable of the level of seething heat his stare can generate. We've been tight, since we hit the Orientation Barracks. He might not accept me so easily in Brooklyn, but here, I am an ideal friend. I like him, though he is headed for trouble that isn't my business.

Now, Morris is a white guy, who comes from a tiny place that apparently is mighty isolated. His behavior is that of a kid that cannot accept anything outside of his limited experience. He is a complete racist and oblivious to the fact that few people share his level of arrogant separatism.   At least most of the troops here know better than to openly act out on this topic. Not Morris, he expands on this crap to anyone who will listen. The racism is not shocking to me, at all.   Change was coming slow as ever, to myself as well as everyone else. I never pretended to be anything but a white guy learning about a new world. Integration in NYC was far from done, and not entirely peaceful. The actions I had seen in the South were filled with frightening images of hate and courage. The big difference between the North and South was the overtness of the separatism. By this time in America, most people hid the racism they held. Not Morris.

Now, Horace was such an unusual fellow that I regarded him as a science project. Drafted from Panama, which already had my head spinning, he was a five foot square of muscles. He spoke so, slowly, that you fell forward, listening to him. I am pretty sure most of what he would say was not English, and he would talk as long as anyone would listen. I loved him; he was hilariously misinformed about America, in every way. Like Norris, he never had any filter to stop his stream of opinions. He was sure that snow covered the continent from Tennessee to NY, which was the top of the map in his opinion. Never heard of Canada, or Asia for that matter, he was wearing the boots very reluctantly. Having this poor guy in the Army was an abomination. Another Panamanian had attempted suicide by drinking Brasso; they were in no way prepared for the shock of Basic in the U.S. His saving grace was his gentle manner. The Army was adopting him because of it. He did have a problem, and I got in it.

Friday night of week four, came to our upstairs bunks with my three actors caged too close. Norris and Morris were having a discussion, something along the lines of "Segagashun is crimnul, y'all makin' nuthin' but sum trubbuh, Norris," I was sitting on my top bunk squirming. Norris was slurring his words, like a viper; he was beyond my control, altogether, "Yocrackr, imma bus you, Shudufucup." What stupendous level of unawareness that Morris had reached I do not know. I had already told him over and over, that all his rants were senseless and dangerous. He looked to me, now, to make more trouble by asking me to back him. This was flat stupid, worse yet, it seemed to be the last straw for Norris. He grabbed Morris and threw him into one of the foot lockers. I never budged, why should I ? There was no question that justice would be done, and now, here comes Horace. Yelling at Norris.

Of course, Morris and Norris had no idea what Horace was angry about. Morris made an immediate, White Boys Gotta' stick together plea to me. He would never understand how pitiful that was, or that he had an ally in Horace. After my long study of Horace. I knew he had a ton of racist attitudes about everyone and everything, and he made Morris look enlightened. He hated, Norris for being Norris, in every way. He identified with the Old South completely and was giving a short and incoherent speech before jumping my homeboy.

He said, and I quote, " Tha,his dalas ,an fina time feryou, ta goagunst moss, noss" The "last and final" part was the key note in understanding that action would follow. Horace used that phrase to mean the very tops, like, "This eggs are dalas an fina."

As many times before, I felt as if I were an observer above a Petri dish, but no time for measurements.

For a moment, I considered letting the whole thing go. Then, as that was unacceptable. I hit Horace on top of the head with my canteen. That, Army type canteen has an edge where it is formed, and that made a nice slice, in the nearly bald dome of my man Horace. Norris and Morris, looked over at the blood and stopped fighting, well, Norris stopped pounding Morris, anyway.

   Now, I had three problems, Morris, Norris, and Horace. I felt pretty proud of this in a creative way. I had managed to get in trouble for Racism, Lack of Racism, and the Canteen Thing, which was most superlative if you ask me. What we had there was a failure to communicate.   I love to help.

Chapter Twenty-Eight: Mercy and Respect

October of 1969, Fort Jackson, South Carolina

Basic Training Mike, Rank E-1

We've been down here at the bottom of Tank Hill for five weeks. Since the quick trip
after my Induction at Fort Hamillton in Brooklyn, on September 11th, these Old
training barracks have been home. The last crummy box, on the bottom of crummy box
hill. The very top of the hill has the " Ponderosa" where they sell the near beer: 3/2
beer they call it.   Reduced alcohol so you cannot get so drunk. Believe me, you don't
have to get very drunk to act out there. We got to go, for the first time, last weekend
after four weeks of training and confinement to the Company Area. You never walk in
the Company Area, trainees run everywhere. By this time, we are indifferent to
running, or physical exertion, the Company is, in Shape. We chant and run, squat and
chant, crawl and sing, " We like it, We love it, We want more of it." The regimen of
early rising , running, and Physical Training every day whips 19 year olds into top
condition, in very little time. Those still struggling with the running, or failing to qualify
with weapons, will be "RECYCLED." This was before today's meaning of, all eco
friendly.   Recycled, meant going to, special training unit, for another 8 weeks of
humiliation. I had managed to overcome my mental weakness at the start, to be
bouncing around like a Tigger. My friends, Bob and Bob, always kept every thing light.
One was from Evanston Illinois, a smiling, Marching Band- Pot head, the other a grizzly.
He looked like he had a beard after shaving, Brooklyn Pothead. We sometimes ran
backwards, when the Drill Instructor, Willie McKnight wasn't looking. I had been
driving the D.I. crazy since day one. His constant ragging on me was a joy for all, and a
bolster to my efforts to deviate in any way possible. I always behaved like his favorite
failure, and he never failed to give me the attention that is so characteristic of Basic
Training Folklore. Many New Yorkers have played this role in Basic, apparently, people
have ideas about NY values. We played our parts with elan'. McKnight would gather
the platoon before the weekends, and ask if anyone had a problem or was thinking of
going AWOL. No one in their right mind would answer, the silence was only a doorway,
for me to enter.

"Well, Sarge,..." I would begin, Never expecting to finish. McKnight would commence to threaten my life, and condemn my New York Soul and Ass to a 'soon to be' VietNamese Hell and Leeches. This routine became a source of great expectation in our platoon. After my surviving a first day, "Hell Day" at the Company Area, when I almost quit, or did quit, about five times, I had become the Star Whipping Boy in the Unit. Every troop looked to me for action, on the idiot front. I would not have made it through that first day without the specific help of the Master Drill Instructor. He literally came to my rescue, deflecting some abuse, that was coming my way. I had fallen to the ground near the steps to the Headquarters with a couple of D.I.'s chasing me, when he cut me a break. He stood over me, encouraging me, telling me not to quit, which I was, and the respite gave me the chance to recover my wits. The man was a towering Viet Nam Veteran, with a Mt. Rushmore type noggin, and a voice from that other mountain, where Moses stood. Among the men doing the training, Master Sargeant Robinson was more than revered. He would occasionally, yell at me, across the Company, "Don't BOLO Shnodder" making everyone laugh. This BOLO, meant failing to qualify with the M-16, that would ruin the running joke of how quick they were sending me to Nam. For me the BOLO would mean a Recycle, a worse fate than Nam. Lastly, all of the Staff in Carolina have tremendous drawls, making my name, Shnodder. Pretty soon, all the recruits are calling each other dickhead and slurring their speech. Basic works your mind, you change, even if, you are aware of it. I had adjusted, and I had shot expert with the M-16. Week six was something I could handle, when my coughing got very much worse. I felt weaker by the hour, boom, boom, sick call, hospital, pnuemonia. The Hospital held me five days and rightly so. My lungs just faded. I couldn't smoke and I dropped weight. Conditioning meant nothing to this disease. And now.

The fifth day inside, I discover that missing a full week of training will be a recycle, Holy Jesus in heaven, that is not happening to me. I began my begging with the Doctors and nurses. "Let me out," I cried all day, and they did. This was a testament to my ability to pester, which is massive, and the tiny value the Army places on trainees. My release, early in the morning, 6 A.M. allowed me to hitch a ride to my Company for Formation. The Doctor gave me a "Profile," meaning a limited duty slip to hand carry. With this profile, I had it knocked. Nobody could make me run, or any other strenouous training. My reunion with the Company would allow my completion of Basic; that was the goal.

The Jeep driver had me jump out at the very far end of our Company Street. The Whole Company was in formation, the Master on his reviewing stand. A silence already in place, as I begin walking toward my platoon, carrying my profile in my hand.

I am very weak, but happy to be back. The distance between the Stand and myself is about 50 meters, defined by my own platoon, standing at attention, the whole distance - asphalt. Now, the Master Sargeant calls my name, loud,

  "Snodder, Priiivate Shnodderr, get down and crawl your useless self over here. You walkin' in my area, BOY" Nobody is laughing, this is going very wrong, as I get down and crawl. The idea that I would yell back at Robinson is ridiculous, I prefer death. The crawl is difficult. You might think it embarassing, as well, but it is not, only much too slow because of my weakness.   I hope nobody thinks I am dogging it. Damn, it is a hard crawl.

   The Company goes on with the morning business. Thankfully, punishments are so common that they hardly get noticed.   My journey concludes at the stand and I stand at attention, awaiting instruction, breathing as much as I can, which isn't much.   The Master Sargeant looks down and signals me, to rejoin McKnight and the boys. Before he can look back to his Company, I hand him my Profile, his face shows exactly what I expected. He sees the level of respect that my crawl has given. Without a word, I do an "about face" and run back to my place. Mercy Accepted and Respect Given.

Chapter Twenty-Nine: Fear in San Antonio

Late November, 1969, San Antonio, Fort Sam Houston

Medical Corpsman Training for me. The alternative to being Infantry for draftee Mike. Something in the Army Placement exams made me a selection for this job. When I got the orders, at the end of Basic, I was happy for a split second, before the fear took over. Mostly every troop drafted would like to avoid Advanced Infantry Training, at least to have any Military Occupational Skill other than Grunt. There is no crying about it; we all know the deal. We're on the fast track to Nam'. At that, it is always nice to think you are getting a golden ticket to some tit job in Hawaii.

The fear of the Medic job is well and truly inside anyone with a brain. One of the most dangerous positions you can be put in, and challenging to the mind on many levels. There is a chance you'll become a Hospital Worker, but mainly, the Infantry is where you are heading.

Fort Sam is a good bit better than most Army bases, the Hospital here is World Class. Our training is serious. Though the Camp Bullis Armadillo chasing is a classic Army joke. They tell you specifically, NOT to chase them. The instant trainees arrive, they begin chasing them and get bitten. Otherwise , the place is pretty serious. We cover all manner of Medical issues, especially field expedient, trauma care. Intravenous and Intramuscular Injections, as well as, raising a weal subcutaneously. Much is stressed about pressure dressing wounds. The guys are mostly absorbing it all without any problem. The fear is there now, in a new way. A deep seated fear in every man here, for the "class" we dread is pending. Fellows begin looking for support from their buddies, but, butt.

I met two actual cowboys here, Mole and Owlly, they were for real buckaroos and had the gashed noggins to show for the Bull Riding. Plenty of the guys here had volunteered to be Medics, signed up for it, knowing the risk. One fellow was a College Champ wrestler. By Gum, they all had that same deep seated fear now.

Yes, the insructions on using a rectal thermometer are the 'real' terror in this group. The joking and teasing about this are nonstop. The thought of this being done by all of us, to all of us, in the large wide open lab rooms is horrifically funny. Hardly an hour goes by without this degrading, creepy chatter, and now many have a pact with a good friend to 'engage' them.

None of those pacts will be honored, the instructors are not new. We will be paired randomly and poker and pokee will exchange places. Needless to say the actual assaults are quite uneventful, though the room is full of the oddest noises you will ever hear from a bunch of 19 year olds.   This story may tickle you, I hope, but it also shows how far along we were on our fall into War. Within weeks, I would be in Asia, and not in any Hospital. I never did get to use THAT skill.

Medic Chapter One: X2B3

January, 1970, Beginning my Trip

After completing Medical Training at Fort Sam Houston in Texas, I traveled home to NYC for a short ' leave'. The weather was bitterly cold, and the first night back, I went sleigh riding with friends in Forest Park. We drank our Southern Comfort until we fell over in the snow.

Though it might seem a time for fun, or special events to be remembered, I only wanted this time to be over. I had long since resigned myself to getting killed in Nam', and anything of value, only confused and saddened me further. I am not sure if I felt depressed about feeling sad, or was sad about my depression. The weight of the situation was even difficult for those around me. Looking at the faces of my Mom and Dad, was torture. Their loveable little child was sinking away , into the worst place, in the world How they suffered ! I made quick work of my leave, and traveled west, to get shipped out.

They were moving troops to Nam' through a Hanger / Factory Building. While I was there some guys scammed me out of 20 bucks, in a card game swindle. To say I had nothing to lose, was an understatement; what kind of scumbubbles pull tricks on fellows here ?

After a 24 hour wait, my 'Mission' was called to the Airfield, to board an Airliner. The troops were transferred by civilian airplanes. My flight would be called... X 2 B 3 . "Mission X 2 B 3".   I immediately sought meaning in this name. What fate was sealed by this Alpha Numeric ? My mind always puzzled about fate. I became more gloomy steadily, with a touch of manic growing slowly. Proceeding with caution is my nature, now being undermined by fatalism. How much can you really worry, about getting killed, before you just " throw your hands in the air, like you do not care"?

The Asia, of our Nam', is a hell of a long way, even from California. Fourteen hours in the air and a couple more on Guam, I think. They told us, Hawaii too; we never got off, so it might have been anywhere, and I did not care. I sat next to a guy, who only wanted to get back to his unit, near Dak To. Obviously, he was nuts. The guys he served with would mostly have gone home. That did not matter; he just could not hack life, stateside. He was a nice little fellow, I was sure he'd be killed; he thought so, too. He was perfect company for me. My mind was most certainly not right, but the idea of this returnee and his sad desire calmed my concerns about insanity. This insanity was not mine, I was only caught in it.

Medic Chapter Two: Manchu Troops

Company A, Third Platoon, Fire Base Rhode Island, Republic of Viet Nam. 1970

Before me, these fellows became the field troops of the 25TH Infantry. I walk in the door, so to speak, as if there is a door. Firebase Rhode Island is FB - Red Dirt in Bags

I meet, Lt. Theodore Pytash, a Pennsylvanian. He looks unaffected by the situation. Being the Platoon leader seems like a natural state of affairs. About 5' 10", he stands on his jungle boots like they are attached to the red dust of this forsaken place. Way too smart to be here, Pytash is right at home. I am feeling awful until we meet, now 10 percent better.

There are three Squad leaders: Reis, Thomas, and Donny. Sarge Reis is like this:

This man is a little too old, for this place; he is not real big, with no extra flesh on a hardened, baked body. His head is large already, and the big nose is way out front. I automatically hate him. He is a great soldier, I hate that, and he knows I am a slacker, immediately. We nod, and he warns me about being, me. I give 'joe army', "the look."

Thomas and Donny, sure did not look like this before Nam. They are ingrained with the shadow of dust, red, wrinkled, squinting, hard, swimming in their jungle fatigues. One hundred and fifty pounds of muscle and anger, wrapped in smiles and jokes. One has the red hair he came in country with, atop his gnarled frame, the other was probably a blonde before the sun and clay got to him; now he is monochrome rust.

The Grunts are sitting on ammo boxes loading up for a mission, they look like this:

Jim Boy, is a straight haired, blond boy, who is washing his fatigues, Ramplain tells me he never changes to new ones, " Bad Luck" Jim is so skinny, his teeth are leading his face toward me.

Gainer, is a tiny troop from the south. His dark skin is topped with a mop of curly, Black-on-black curls. He looks like he has seven parents contributing. Next to him is Chanon, a for-real Chicano, who is 5' 5" and chubby, which is super odd. As a weight loss program, humping the bush is effective; the average weight of these guys is...160 or less. Chanon has the mustache going around his mouth, in almost a full circle. He grumbles constantly, in a mix of languages. He is not happy to be put upon, unlike Gainer who is a cheerful Mickey Mouse; Chacon is the dwarf Grumpy. Later, I will see these two walk out into the rubber trees, under full packs. Gainer carries the

Radio, and Chanon is the packiest packer ever. They hunch over to carry the loads, with their heads protruding far in front. In their green outfits, they are like turtles.

Crackie B. Crackwell is here. This ass belongs here. Southern boys can make you feel like you 'never had a clue about anything' that they know. Crackie B. knows about everything. His best buddy is Okie, so you can imagine what they think of a...brand new, NYC Medic.

Crackie, is as tall as I am and rail thin; his beard grows fast; he sunburns too. The whitest skin and the blackest hair, the slyest grin, and the slangest accent, he is South of the Southern South. Okie is a stumpy guy, with the rust overwhelming any features. Both go straight to rattling my cage, another time this might have gone wrong, but I am so upset at being here they seem to sense it. They are the heart of this Platoon, and the new Medic is adopted.

Ramplain and Moose stick together, all the time; they are a nuisance to everyone until Moose says to stop. More light skinned, dirty blonde boys, from Pennsyvania and Ohio, they are opposites physically. Moose carries the M-60 Machine Gun and Ramplain carries the Ammo Belts, One has the height, the other the muscle. Moose is as kind and friendly as Ramplain is mean and stupid.

There is a guy, named WOP ! That's his name; he doesn't got another. He looks like someone from a pirate ship; has hair is so, black and swarthy, that it resembles a bandana. He has a beard on the side of the face that he just finished shaving. He snickers and talks of atrocities. Everyone tells him to "shut up", and he never does. His name IS WOP. Sorry.

There is a sniper with them, Maroquez. Multi-tour Maroquez. Oh, yeah, sniper! He was here to get high, as much as possible. People were afraid to go in the field next to him. The perfect picture of the sneaky junkie, with an M-14, and a Sniper Scope. He sniffled and cowered, like he was back on the block.

I met Jacksus; they sent me to the perimeter to help him burn shit. I thought it was a pot joke. Walking closer to the Perimeter was not my idea of fun, but Reis told me to go, so, off to burn shit with Jacksus.

You know, now that I think of it, I learned a lot in a short time meeting Jacksus.

First, when you are enclosed, in a War Zone circle - you have to burn the shit. Use Fuel and Stir; it's that simple. Second, there are things worse than being in Viet Nam.

Third, you can pretty much do...whatever else you want, if you are willing to burn the shit.

Jacksus was a Chicago guy. Drafted, black, and angry before all these reasons to be angry; he was my kind of people. The Company Commander was holding him in the rear, for various offenses, some quite real. He had a fun way of speech, and an inside knowledge of power and corruption, which he shared readily. He could have gone back to Second Platoon in a minute, if he wanted to knuckle under, instead, he burned the shit. Choice is yours, my friends?

I had yet to go outside the Firebase as, the new Doc.

Medic Chapter Three: First Days

The Area West of Saigon, RVN.   1970

First Days, Michael G. Schneider, Platoon Medic, 25th Infantry

February, I am here grimacing, at the results of me failing to dodge. Viet Nam, Third day, moved to 25th Infantry Headquarters. Only stayed a full day...in Bien Hoa. Getting assigned to a medical company, or more likely an Infantry company, soon. Killing time, moping, new guy, stupid and witless. Under a metal roof, screened walls, sandbagged at the base. Thinking that this shack is pretty rudimentary; it will be looked on as way in the rear within days!

Troop comes in, not a new guy, "anybody wanna get high!" Really good idea, huh? If you were in your right mind, you would never consider doing it.   I went right out with the guys smokin'.   Hit, Hit . . . Wow, this is good pot, so fast. Hit again, man, I am lit and, now, standing right in front of me, is the Top Sarge! I still have the joint in my mouth, god, this pot is strong ! Things are a little foggy as he takes me to the office. Sitting on a chair, just me and the Top, and he is pissed, and. . . he has a Big 45 pistol in his hand. He says to me, for real, "It's guys like you who are destroying this war!"   I am still high, and maybe he is thinking of shooting me; nevertheless, I am very proud to be so honored.

This moment of special attention results in me, getting sent to my Infantry Company, with a letter of condemnation from the Top, to the Company Commander. He is a West Pointer on a second tour, crew cut, field hard guy. Carries the AR-15. the chopped version of the standard M-16. He might kill me, for all I know. He makes it clear, I am not a welcome addition to his troop. More and more, spouting intimidating crap. I am already in Nam' and expect to die in Nam', only my platoon will judge me ! I know they will call me "Doc" and trust my commitment to save them, under any circumstances. Even new medics know what the deal is gonna be. Put simply, when the shit gets bad,   really bad, they are gonna' call your name, MEDIC, and you will, GO!

I go to meet my platoon; Lt. Pytash, Platoon Leader with Donny, Reis, and Thomas as his sarges, moving the crew of guys named, moose, champy, gainer, jim b. , and many more with names of grunts. Everyone seems as ready to meet me, as they can be. I am replacing a...legend ! JONAS, Doc Jonas, the best medic, most heroic, and worthy person. What is worse, he truly is, all that. The Company Commander, made him the C.P. medic, which means, he stays with the boss in the field. I get Third Platoon. This time I am not so special !

Before my arrival, I had no idea what a Firebase might be, or what a pile of dirt could amount to, - Firebase Rhode Island. The biggest things there were some Artillery pieces. About everything else was made of sandbags and covered with metal culvert, or con ex boxes, big metal corrugated shipping containers. The red dust was terrific; it seemed to turn even the troops red. The perimeter was a line of bunkers, dug into a bermline, which is nothing but a pile of dirt. Just outside the berm was the barbed, and concertina, and razor wire, sitting atop all manner of explosives and flammables, like foo gas. Maybe we had some White Phosphorus rigged up too! Like a big party, waiting for human wave attacks, or sappers, the sneaky guys. The whole place was like a circle, and seemed quite small, facing the huge rubber plantation, across the dirt road.

It held the rear areas for the Manchu' Battalion, 4/9 Infantry, and some artillery batteries. Alpha and Bravo Companies were in base, at the time. I had already been to Bien Hoa, Cu Chi, Bear Cat, and been equipped with an Aide bag, M-16, ruck sack, web belt, jungle fatigues, etc. As far as training on Infantry operation, I had none. I didn't know all the things that they teach because I was ten weeks becoming a medic, instead of taking Advanced Infantry Training. Now, I was to learn on the job, as it were. I should say that I was extremely shaky, to the point of paralysis.

As we walked out of the firebase toward the rubbers, on my first mission, the next morning, I asked the radio operator, Gainer, how long we might be gone. He said to expect four to seven days. At this moment, I realized we would be spending the goddam night in the jungle; I was shocked. Honestly, I did not know a single useful thing!

We continued walking through the rubbers, a very orderly stand of trees, none small. Corridors of space, streams and beams of light, and a shutter effect of vision. As you pan, left to right, you see: 500 yards, 20 yards, 10 feet, a tree. It was very tranquil and still, except for the silly amount of noise made by this company of manchu' infantrymen. American troops need much stimulation, to be at their best; we weren't sneaking up on anybody! Of course, each step I took with great caution, actually trying to step on Gainer's footprints. This is because...I am very afraid of very many ideas, and am making this the most dangerous moment, it is not. This very day, we will hump 14 kilometers, and not through orderly rubbers. Half of the time, we chop a path straight into jungle. I walk close enough to the point man, Chanon, to see that he is too tired and frustrated to be appropriately cautious. The day, my first in the field, is long and tiring. We set up what they call a "bushmaster".   I actually pull watch for an hour. Cannot see a thing, and I hear noise right in front of us. Moose says, "it's us, jackass." I thought about how inept I was.

   The next morning, the thinking would stop, and we would begin again, in a new world for Alpha Company!

Medic Chapter Four: Second Days

First Days, 1970, Out in the field. My second day in the boonies.

A full and exhausting day's walk, from FB Rhode Island.

We are up Early; time is by the sun, or geography, or mission related. If you have "the watch", your hour goes by very slowly. My hour last night was, sooo long. I see our bushmaster's position this morning is spread around pretty carelessly; any attack, from any angle, would be big trouble. We mill and mull as the Lt. is giving the sarges the orders for the day. We saddle up, and are ready to hump. . . we move out alright, the radios are crackling, the pace is quick, we are moving! Actually, we are running, in a file through light jungle. I know this is not normal. Then, word filters back down the line. Bravo company's helicopter down. Troops down, Hot?, we do not know, but we are the closest to the rescue, secure, or. . . we don't know.

I am squeezing my aide bag, tight. Running through the jungle, to the crash, we are headlong rushing. There is purpose, desire and no hesitation. Oddly this is way dangerous; there are enemy to consider. But Alpha company does not, and we are close. There is a noise and there is a smell: Fire, Fuel, Jungle. As we arrive, I notice some . . . boom . . . thing, Boom, just before, the chopper explodes into flames.

It is burning less than 30 meters away. We can see through the light forest, as we approach. Closer now, the chopper itself is upright, almost as if it landed. Sadly and horrifically, it contains the flight crew! We do not know how many infantry men from Bravo were aboard. A full Huey might have a dozen people total. Looking down at the ground next to me, I see a chunk of burning red and black metal. To my right there is a grunt from bravo, sitting against a tree. He is in shock, can't speak. Doc' Jonas tells me to check him out. As he is not injured, I wander forward a bit. It is soon evident that nobody survived this crash and explosion. The remains of the fallen Bravo troops are changing the lives of us all ! The flight crew sits in their chopper, unable to help themselves, or us. We cannot even approach their tormented forms. Many of my company, are shocky. The heroic Jonas cries, along with many others. Plenty of troops have fanned out, to secure the crash site. There is no rescue. We think there were as many as Thirteen people on the chopper.

I return to my shocked troop by the tree. He, and a couple of others from Bravo, jumped from another chopper, before we arrived. I can see he is still very shaky. Glancing back toward the debris burning near him,   I see the 'black and red metal' has stopped burning. It is not metal, it is the reason this troop is ruined. He was approaching when the explosion occurred, and was hit by this piece... of Bravo Company, like himself ! The accumulation of facts and figures at this scene is beginning to make me lose touch. I am trying to react normally; this trooper has done just that! This is not normal. We are none of us the same.

My platoon is assigned security. The site is light jungle, but far from the space needed for this recovery. People get to work clearing an LZ, for choppers. Blessedly, I do not do the body recovery. To those who did that work, my thanks and my sorrow. Your Bravo fellows needed the help to get home!   This story is real; many lives that day were stopped or restarted. Sincere apologies to those who loved the lost, of this day. Perhaps the way we ran to save them, will be a reminder, that they were worthy .

My emotional life was changed forever by the time we spent, the day and the night, with this event   and those troops.

Choppers came the next morning to retrieve those men. Sadly, incongruently, and coldly, they carried a hot breakfast on the way out. I suppose the rear knew, we were in an intolerable situation, but there was little appetite. Nobody was unaffected. The young man by the tree, never recovered. He was sent home, but not for two months.

Bravo and Alpha Companies had more troubles later, more than once. By that time, nothing had a genuine impact on me. I had gone to Viet Nam thinking that I would die. As time passed, survival seemed, more likely. But, as of that day and night in the field with Company A, third platoon, my soul was never the same.

Medic Chapter Five: Eagle Lift

Come With Me, on this Eagle Lift. 1970, April, FB Rhode Island, RVN

We are going out this morning, that much we know. I am your Platoon Medic. You are a Rifleman, named Mo. We came "In Country", five weeks ago, and you stay close to me for luck. Our luck has been pretty awful up til now, and I am not a happy guy.

Our Platoon is headed for the "Straight Edge," first trip there for you and me. Our platoon is out in the boonies so much they have names for the areas they hit. We got resupplied last night, and have cleaned fatigues. Your "new shirt" has a name tag: "Haggelstrack". Our jungles fatigues are well worn, that's good. You want nothing new, these reused ones are lucky. Neither one of us has a haircut, since we arrived, you shaved while we were at FB Rhode Island. Our Rucksacks are full; mine is about half the size of yours. The Ammo and frags that you are carrying, are banded around you, over the wraps of 60 ammo belts, for the Machine gun. We have water for four days, and food for five or six. We both carry M-16's' we have Steel Pots on our heads. We have dry socks and underwear; these are absorbing the sweat of a 93 degree morning.

Tree lined to the North, Fire Base Rhode Island is mostly surrounded by rubber trees. The Chopper Pad is , just red dirt , flat, crushed, and plowed months before. We wait by the berm line, until the Birds are In bound and close. When the Choppers are on the deck, waste no time.

Radios crackle up, and we move out, crossing the 200 meters of Landing Zone, and securing the woodline. Three Birds with First Cav. Insignia, pop over the tree tops. Swooping forward toward the field at first, they begin to lean backward, slowly. This changes their speed, and seems to bring them to the ground like ducks, extending the skids like feet. Naturally, the red dirt loves this; if we were clean, that is over. My squad is assigned to second chopper, the Lieutenant's in first. The rotors never slow, we move onto the silver deck platform, seats in the middle, or plop our butts, near the wide open doorway. Both of us, are hanging our legs out of the right side, next to a 'Door Gunner'. WE, are still human; HE is a 'Gunner', though he might actually be, Haggelstrack. We no longer have personhood, just a grunt, and a 'Gunner' and a Doc'. Our bird tilts forward, and gives a slight dip, following his brother just ahead. We slide back a bit, as the Chopper leans into the wind and rises. Not Too High, now, they only need tree-top level, and we skim, narrowly, above the rubbers, at the west end of the Chopper Pad.

We are now westbound, toward the Straight Edge. The greenery is less than five feet from our dangling boots. Our speed is terrific, when gauged by this ocean of leaves, waving below. The safety of the low level flying is the difficulty for enemy guns to target us. Although you look mesmerized by the beauty and power, by the oddity, and the stirring noise, by the wind and the action, I am just scared, unhappy, and worried about hitting the "Hot LZ", by the Straight Edge. There is never any way to know if Army Intelligence has actually...hit the jackpot, and picked the exact spot where you can get shot! They try, that's for sure.

As we leave the Airspace above the Rubbers, our pilots climb. The scrubby drylands below offer no cover, and we see the actual straight edge. The contrast is movie-like. Once the border of a Giant Rubber Plantation, this line in the Jungle survives as a monument, and a "No Mans Land." The Boys of Alpha Company do NOT like the "Straight Edge". Of course, the Bo Lois, and The Hobos, are just as bad, Haha! Let's get these Choppers on the Deck, Huh ?

We are ready to flee the birds as they descend. "Just get away from the damn birds," the gooks are gonna' shoot at the birds, first, last, and always!

Once again, but with way more force, the Choppers move forward and ease back, more like Buck back, to slow and flop, for a brief moment. The Door Gunner opens up on the woodline with his mounted M-60, making it impossible for us to know whether anyone is firing AT us.   SO, we open up on the woodline, as we bounce out. Before we can know what the hell is going on, the birds are on their way back to clean sheets. They must feel great. I am sick, you...are firing short bursts, and securing the woodline, with Boy and Ruggles. The only ones firing are, US, whew! not the Hot.

You turn to tell me, like you always do, "I told You, Dic." You are the only one who won't call me 'Doc'. BUT, I went home, 45 years ago. See ya' Mo.

Medic Chapter Six: Up the Hill Manchus

April of 1970, Alpha Company, 4/9 Manchu Battalion. Out in the Field, West of Saigon.

The whole damn Company is trooping along, up hill, toward a suspected position of a dug-in Regiment of NVA soldiers. This is the mission plan, we have our orders. Up we go to engage a force approximately ten times our size.   Dreadful to think that Army Intelligence might actually be correct. They must not even take themselves seriously.

We have constantly been chasing this ghost Regiment; it does not exist in the way the Super Staff in the rear imagines. NVA don't stumble around in crowds and make noise like us. Their plans don't include exposing themselves to U.S. firepower at all. They understand the game.

Grunt Units like us, straight leg units that walk around understand, as well. Our callous overlords expose us as much as possible. This does have a purpose besides getting Infantry killed; the idea is to find and maintain contact with enemy forces. Then, we can bring the hell that is Air Support, upon the Landscape. This works, but not well, If the other team would only behave like pop up targets and stop all this moving and hiding. By 1970, we had reduced the Regular Army of North Viet Nam to scraps. They had learned every lesson about fighting this type of conflict. They were going to hunker down and murder us, then flee. They tunneled and ambushed, strategically. With little to waste, they became efficient. Hunting them was a new sport for the big units of the U.S.; we had a lot to learn.

So, anyhow, up we trudged.   A long line of Alpha grunts, my Platoon walking point. Chanon on point as usual, he took point a lot and he was never any good at it. Moose behind, with Okie. They were the machine gun team, behind Okie was Fireball 3-6. He was our Lieutenant and then Mario, lazy, hazy Mario, right in front of me. I didn't think medics ever walked so far up the line, but I always humped behind Mario and liked to stay close to 3-6. Fireball and Mario were an odd couple, but great guys. They had nice awareness on the move. We were kind of "getting into position walking" rather than assaulting the place. The high ground where the "Big To Do" was scheduled was still half a click away. If you could be more relaxed about things, I don't know how. The mission was a huge cluster, the Top Sarge was along, the Company Commander was asking for constant updates. Big deal, it was; we, up front, were not so hyped. It was a nice dry day, not too hot and there was ample shade and light brush. We were strolling in front of a hyperbole prone group of Boss types, a helicopter with the Battalion Colonel and lifers who wanted a body count. This made us go extra slow.

In our three months in the area, we had never had a serious firefight. Day after day, we had been trolled around as lures, and had not blundered into anything deadly. We were not very well tested at all. As we humped, the lead elements stepped over a log across the trail. Chanon and Moose and Okie, I could see them. Fireball next, and then Mario. Lazy Mario decides to sit down straddling the damn thing. Soon as he did he smacked his neck and yelped; the cutter ants got him, I thought. I was only a step away, something bit my face next to my eye. That made me slap myself and knock my glasses off. It hurt, but I was laughing about Mario being so lazy, until I rose to find myself covered in swarming angry bees, being stung so many times that I opened my mouth to scream, and in went the Bees. They were big and fuzzy bees, I can tell you that, and crunchy. I had handfuls to push and crush, as I ran back toward my Company. In such a terror, I dropped everything: my rucksack, my weapon, the Aide Bag. I had a thought of my Mother because death seemed imminent. Quite a distance back, the Top Sarge had popped a bunch of smoke grenades; these subdued the Bees.

Lots of troops had arrived there and had been stung badly. Basically, my Company had been routed by a bunch of insects. Mario was worse than anybody, he and I had dozens of stingers in our heads. Luckily we were not swelling. Two guys with two or three stings were in bad shock, and swollen like all hell. Altogether, nine of us were evacuated. As the chopper rose, the wind made all my stings hurt all over again. Those Bees were vicious, maybe they were NVA.

Up front of the log, as soon as he saw our torment, Okie told the Point element to sit down and be still. They never got stung. I still wonder about this day and the Bees that wiped us out. Maybe they saved us, huh ?

Medic Chapter Seven: GPS Foibles

Early GPS, Year 1970, SOMEWHERE Out On Your Borderline

Come, Along for a walk with Third Platoon, Company A, 4/9 Infantry. Seemingly, way far away from our Rear Echelon friends, but, secretly accompanied by an eager Artillery Battery, at a Fire Base, about three miles to the West. Well, everything is to our west, because we are working the Cambodian Border and we are not permitted to encroach upon it.

We are moving, quite a bit more than suits us; the Military Intelligence is getting into the Act. Having us, on the move, is exactly the same as trolling a fishing lure past the snags and sand bars, hoping to get a crafty lunker to strike. If you asked the "planners", they would never admit this, but the evidence is overwhelming. Among the reasons, we understand this notion, is that we are Ambushing when we are not moving, as if we are predator and prey, depending on what the Army decides. As time goes by, in the conflict, our side is becoming slightly less idiotic. The troops have always wanted to do the "right thing", and recently the Army is, wising up, a bit. Another obvious clue that our movements were part of the fun, was the Artillery and Air Support Units constant interest in our whereabouts. This brings me to our... GPS-Cave Style.

When you go humping the boonies with the grunts, you have to do Land Navigation. This is accomplished by strictly following an azimuth and measuring the distance traveled along that imaginary line. This is completely, No Joke. Your position, " in it's exactness" could become a real crucial topic. I would prefer an expert to fill you in on the more sophisticated aspects. We counted paces anytime a significant move was ordered. A simple task for a person otherwise unencumbered, hehe. I actually counted a couple of times myself, and I did OK. When the moves were a couple of Kilometers, both the count and the azimuth might get muddled. After all, the terrain was pretty much boonie.

Interestingly, and usefully, an Artillery Battery can place their shells very specifically, and without our direction. If we wanted a "Marking Round" exactly on a set of coordinates, it was done, without fanfare. They can make the rounds explode at a height, that makes them easily visible. You might have guessed already, that we did not like to do that. The rounds were like the bell on the cat. Not that the VC would not know where you were anyway. Let me sum it up. If we were confident about our Ambush location, we would never call in anything else but the coordinates. Were we shaky in the whole thing, we would pre- schedule, with Marking Rounds, as much "H.E.

on the deck", as possible. This way, we could call the Arty Fire Mission immediately, and on the ground with High Explosive rounds, if, IF, you know.

  So, this dry , crispy, sweaty, boring, Four Klick, humping day, on the diddy over here, Foibles was counting the paces. If you had been around me, in the bush, you knew that I was the biggest, second guesser, ever.   The idea that a guy named Foibles was counting, gave me the creeps, so I tried to keep count, as well.   On the way, my mind wandered to Basketball, and gone was the count. That did not stop me from telling 3-6, my Platoon leader, that Foibles was off, by 400 paces. I just wanted the "Marking Round". Hey, I wanted it. Our ambush site reminded me of a gully wash from The Lone Ranger. No Bandito would set up here; I wanted to move to the rocks above which, there was no 'rocks above'.   I was hinky, that's all.

  For sure, 3-6 felt the same.   Before we even dropped our rucksacks, he was on the PRC- 25 radio with the Arty, who were drooling over our position. They had us less than 200 meters from the border, which they could draw in the sky. We would be able to see their 'Marker' just to the West and slightly South. The round would define our position and give away nothing.   We stood facing the West, awaiting the rush and clapping sound. Ready and able, the Arty shot. ssssssssh, POP, we jumped a bit at the sound, BEHIND us, about three hundred meters !   Back to Viet Nam we hustled, like mice, when the lights come on. I wonder what Foibles was thinking about when he took five hundred extra paces, three hundred of 'em in Cambodia.

Medic Chapter Eight: Hit and Run Cambodia

May, 1970, Cambodia, with the 25th Infantry

Hitting and Getting Hit.

They got us running everywhere. The First Cav is the fork and we are the spoon. Chasing the COSVN rear, supposedly the Big Boss of the VC, and NVA headquarters. After a few weeks of this, it seems true. Supplies and rear area troops are readily discovered on a bunch of big trails. The trails are like highways, in a primitive and camoflaged way. Some ridiculous scenes pop up, because we are so unexpected here. After all, we avoided the border for years, respecting the imaginary jungle line. My platoon was always nervous anywhere near it.

A dry path into a deeply wooded area took my platoon into a quiet, triple canopy world of trouble.

The aerial recon to the North of our Companies' position reported activity, possibly major activity. The top rankers were still hoping for some jackpot capture of the Ho Chi Pentagon. The idea was a joke among the field troops; the construction in this place was sticks and stones, and scarce on the stones. No matter what we think, Infantry Platoons do not get an opinion, off we go in search of major trouble. Another platoon, 25 troops, if you count me, looking for a Regiment to fight. This trail was a small one, obviously being used regularly. Even a few days will allow the jungle to show you disuse. We were working it serious, hand signaling and taking care about our noise discipline. The boys were getting good at all things sneaky. I was walking, 20 meters back, in front of our drag. Whoa !

Hand up, clenched, down and quiet, we got something. Later, I heard the point had seen two NVA, sitting on the edge of a bunker. Got them unaware, and called our halt. We had time to get the M-60 up front, before opening up. . . And we," blew the bush". but. . . the 60 misfired, alerting the bunker and spoiling our advantage. The rest of the riflemen, opened up and a plentiful amount of ammo went down range. While this went on, I got called to the front, "just in case," they told me. Everybody was already laughing, and ragging on me, for complaining. They knew I hated to move for no reason. Some fire was coming back, I 'm pretty sure, but it was not near our level. I did not even consider firing, the situation was under control.

We made no progress, and the opposition was stiffening. In a minute, I was worried and the boys were getting busy. Killer asked if he could throw a grenade. Killer always wanted to throw his grenades, and always wanted more action. He was an idiot, and lots of fun. The jungle was very thick, and the entire scene was in an extremely, tiny area. The bunker was only 20 feet away. Crap! things were getting bad, fast. Lt. said, "fine, Killer," and off went the grenade.   Bang, followed by the most hellacious increase in firing, coming our way. The damn trees were coming down in shredded wood style. We were firing, I was firing for all I was worth. That was a first, with my face stuck to the dirt. Someone said, "Killer, You pissed them off," like shooting at them was Ok, as long as you observe the No Grenade rule.

   And, we laughed some more. We were in Big Trouble. Lt. was on the PRC-25 radio with the Company Commander; the excitement for the contact was evident when they asked if we could "Maintain It?"   Lt. asked if they would like to "speak to the enemy," and added, "we will be overrun shortly." The situation made us hysterical. There was a lot of giggling, about how very buried we were.

   The things that can bail out a U.S. grunt, in this spot are Air support and reinforcement. Our fellow Company platoons one and two, were too far away. Artillery is about the same as Gunships, inside the canopy, real scary. We continued exchanging fire, at a furious pace, without casualty. Even in close quarters, the density is protecting our position, I guess.

   Some Artillery is available, and we bring it. Looks as though the tree lines are making this ineffective, and too close is just that, TOO close. So we stick with the Helicopter Gunships. Two are here, within minutes, and we pop smoke to mark our position. This is silly due to the smoke drifting through the trees. "Nevermind the small talk," Lt. says, "bring the rockets, north of the smoke. "   The Chopper is reluctant, thinking that may hit our position. Lt. is just plain lying to get one run to steer the rest. That may be anywhere, fine, just fire. I hope you never hear such a convesation about rockets. We hunker a tiny bit more, and the rockets bring their shredding top to bottom, across the scene, they bring an awful noise. I have an idea where they struck, Lt. probably knows better. The run did suppress fire a bit on both sides.

   This has all taken between five and fifty minutes, I don't know; we have little idea what is our actual status. We have certainly never taken fire like this. Our own response seems an afterthought. We are tiring and looking to Lt., for action. He provides it, terrifically. Here is how. He calls for the Gunship Run to shift further south, right where we are, and tells us this. "Get down. Soon as this shit hits, get up and diddy mao, Ok?, we are headed south together."   FINE, we are all laughing, and shooting, and calling gunships on our own position.

   Capturing the COSVN rear, we are.

Whoosh, Slashing screeching banging slamming, impact . . . Up, Run . . . we are carrying out the plan. No one is down. I, for one, am almost completely spaced out. We have done it; the firing is gone. We slow, in a semi-clear space. My breath is almost normal. When suddenly, something the size of my face, plops on my nose; focusing back, I see it is an immense spider. I promptly scream, like a little girl. The hysteria breaks loose in everyone, as they see, Doc' flailing to smack his own face.

Lt. is on the radio explaining our "tactics" to the Company Commander; the jerk back there wanted us to stay put. They wanted to find something big, but refused to believe we walked right into it. They have no idea, we had called the gunship in on ourselves. Sometimes you just want to shoot these dopes.

With no casualties and daylight to burn, they send us and second platoon back in. Second Platoon had tried to reinforce us, but got pinned down by the fire coming from our party, 200 meters away. We do not want to go. Now is the time, for the Arty and B-52's, but NO...they need us to gather intelligence. I am a little angry. Back we go. We find this: 200 positions, dug in, supplies, documents, family possessions, the items of life, in a jungle base camp for 500 troops.

We shot at two of them, eek!

They left almost as quickly as we did. They defended until they fled. They must have been rear guard, or new guys, explaining why they fired so much, and hit so little, maybe.

I can say this, calling fire missions on your own position is memorable.

Medic Chapter Nine: Crying in the Rain

May, 1970, Cambodia, Worn Out

Been in the Cambodian Jungle for weeks. So many things are different since we choppered into this new Operation. We have been 'Out in the Field' for 20 days straight, minimum, resupply has been kind of weak, compared with our previous shorter missions. We have plenty of Ammo - we've used quite a bit. A hundred times as much as usual, and everyone is armed to the teeth, even me. The regular grunts are carrying 16 or 20 magazines of M-16 ammo and wraps and wraps of M-60 bullets on belts around their chests and waists. We have loads of Frags and Laws Rockets, and Claymore mines, and smoke Grenades, along with some weapons we've captured. We have captured a lot and blown up some terrific souvenirs, including AK -47 's. We have to travel light; every damn day is a new set of wacky orders and chopper flights. Our heads are spinning; though successful so far, the Incursion is stressful as all hell, and exhausting.

Mostly, the weather has been OK and we have become experienced field troops. Still, we could use a break, some rest, clean fatigues and showers. I am not the only one with a pretty full beard. We are walking down a long, dirt road, as the rain begins. Toward a place where the Engineers and Transit Guys are trying to set up a fire base to support us, as best they can way out here. You can see they have bulldozed up a Bermline on the Perimeter, fresh as a grave and you can smell the tortured earth and vegetation they crushed. There are no structures, only vehicles, large, noisy, diesel, Trucks and Tracks. The crevices and tire ruts are already filling with the increasing rain, which is becoming a torrent.

As we enter, the day is fading and we've had a long one. Across the expanse, about fifty yards, you can see the Mess trucks, and there seem to be some fresh fatigues piled up there, too. The food is not ready; some of the guys walk over toward the fatigues and grab a few, but they are wet, already. The ground is slipping away toward mush and the scene is chaotic. My spirits are falling, and the rain is completely ruining this gallant effort by these support troops.

We decide, on our own, that this is no place for 'straight legs' and walk back out down the same road. Saddled up and slogging, my platoon is drag assin'. To be blunt, I am crying. We do not even have a mission, we're just leaving, walking out to the night, and the night is here.

About a click' outside the Berm, we pull into the woodline and spread out, like a regular ambush, but this is no ambush. Not an order is given, not a Claymore set, and hardly a word spoken. The roadway is a higher than our position, and there is a little cover. As I sink to the place that will be my bed, it is covered with two inches of water. I cry, but no one sees me, Crying in the Rain.

Medic Chapter Ten: Prisoner Exchange

May 1970, Cambodia for the second week.

Very dry and plenty hot, this walk on a huge trail has my Company worried. Not only does the trail show heavy foot traffic, there is also plenty of evidence that trucks plowed through. These would be the other team, moving all manner of stuff. Chasing the "Headquarters of the NVA" is the mission of the Cambodian Incursion, and though we are joking about it, all the time, this Jungle Highway under our boots is not funny. We are stepping on THE Real Ho Chi Minh Trail, a place that was previously a safe haven for Charlie. We are the lead element of a large troop column, Three Platoons of Alpha, a Company sized Operation. 100 Guys.

The trail is wide enough for us to be spread across on either side. Experienced Grunts, spread out left and right with good intervals. The light canopy above has a quieting effect, to the point of hearing the drone of the bugs. I am walking 50 meters back from the point men, yes, men, as two platoons are working the file at one time. Everything about being in Cambodia is unique, and we have never had another platoon walking at our side. The Company Commander is further back, with the drag platoon. So far, it is unsettling, and now, it becomes stark shocking nervous, as the shots ring out, up front.

Riflemen are 'opening up' on something for about fifteen seconds. We throw ourselves down and the cry comes up for Medics. As I run forward, my platoon is waving me goodbye and laughing. I am cursing them and whoever is calling, and Nam and Cambodia specifically. Scared and winded, I arrive at the point where six grunts are hovering over a wounded troop. I plop down at his side on my knees and exclaim, "This is a Goddamn Gook, you jackasses." Hard to even describe how angry this made me. I could have easily gotten killed running up the line while the shit was hitting. Nobody gets up and runs under automatic weapon fire; it is idiocy to do so!

As I begin to stand up, my fellow Medic from first Platoon arrives, and goes to work patching our new friend. Of course, I help because of Tommy being such a friend. I do not want to help this tiny thing, at all. He is the reason I am learning to hate, so damn well. Now, he is shooting at me, and getting shot, and making me run through the jungle and , , , why the hell these stupid grunts did not finish this, I do not know! My friend Tommy and I have stabilized the wounds; there are two and a half gunshot wounds...just don't ask. While we do this, kneeling so very close to this miniscule person, he becomes more real, and human, and pathetic. He is dressed in an NVA uniform. Total weight - 100 starving pounds; Height - almost none. He is missing: a bunch of teeth, shoes, weapons and a silver dollar size piece of his skull. The skull is healed over, with the thinnest of skin, and the thinnest of hair.   Through this, the pulse can be SEEN .

Why,   does it have to be so complicated?   All my time prepping my inhumanity is being undone, and Tommy is not helping. You would think he might at least notice the uniform; honestly, he is a saint.   He stopped carrying a weapon to run faster to his troops. There are a bunch of heroic Medics here; why they gave me the Bag? I do not know.

Now, this is a big mission, OK. Places to go, People to meet, like, not this pitiful little dink.   He does not matter in this spectacular maneuver. We have to DO something, but what ?

In a cleverly worded message, from our Company Commander, he indicates that we should 'complete' this mission!   Here is where I do come in handy; I send back a clever two word reply.   The grunts in this Company are decidedly NOT cold murderers, and for sure, the Medics aren't. I carry a bayonet, as a sidearm, a useless one admittedly. I just like big knives. Our little friend would like me to kill him with it. He gives me the sign, to do so, when he sees my toy. Sort of a compliment to me, I suppose, or revealing how reviled we were by the Viet Nam home team. What a strange feeling came to me, in this moment. There were Grunts with me, who believed IN ME. My Platoon leader, always took my advice on crazy things.   Yes, I got an idea.   This was always trouble!

The Commander was a West Pointer, the Big Brass was all over this Operation, looking to create Glory and Valor, so, Bingo - now, we tell the Chief, " this prisoner has vital intelligence, for sure." Yes, YES, he is probably a High Ranking General. I wish you could see this poor little soul, lain in a stranger manger; he looked so perfectly harmless and innocent.

Fortunately, our heroic West Pointer C.O. , had not even looked at him, which made his 'subtle' suggestion of, finishing him, even more heinous. He bought the story, sold it to the Choppers above, full of Gloryhound Officers, and arranged a Dustoff Helicopter Evacuation, for the guy.   I was happy as a monkey, and went to harangue my platoon about waving goodbyes, the bastards. We got a good distance from where the Chopper was trying to hoist our tiny captive.   Tommy and I were relieved by a crew of grunts, who began putting the guy into a basket which had been lowered through the trees. Things were looking good, as he rose to about twenty feet, THEN, the Goddamn NVA 'opened up' on the Chopper.   I guess, the creeps could not resist. The chopper swooped away, and we returned fire, in every direction. The heat and noise had me flat, face down. Quick as that, it was over.   We "saddled up".   I was angry, and I still am, I was confused; that hasn't changed, either.

 Our prisoner didn't leave with the Chopper, and he wasn't with us.

Medic Chapter Eleven: Beckford's Story

May 1970, Cambodia, with the 25th Infantry.

Night after day, the very last days in Cambodia. We are set up in a field, light woods surrounding this mostly low grass field.

The whole damn company, the C. P. or command post, right in the middle. We dug in, very rare for what seems like a peaceful night. Been quiet for a couple of days. We know we are returning to Cu Chi, our Home. in the near future. The Cambodian excursion filling our last month and a half with action. Oh, we are very different because of it. After the experiences of the past few weeks, my company feels confident about our dominance in combat situations. We have decimated every area we visited. For all the fear and misery, we are thus rewarded. It is a calm and tranquil evening.

Sounds stupid, but we have kicked ass everywhere, inflicted casualties, destroyed supplies, captured prisoners, brought the shootin' war to the so called COSVN rear area, and the last exit on the "Ho Chi Minh Trail". Also, had zero KIA on our side. Dug in and quiet. Claymores out to protect our perimeter, a very dry, calm, still night settled on our confidence. Regular Infantry guarded their own positions. Pulling watch for themselves. Quiet.

THEN , , , shot, shot, shot, maybe a dozen bangs, maybe less. Arisen, the company responded with rounds, down range in every direction. Many hundreds of rounds of automatic M-16. Sleeping, when this popped off, my dopey head peeked toward the woodline, across our set up, and beyond the other side of the perimeter. The original burst came from there; almost thought I could glimpse them as I woke. Of course, my platoon, like all grunts, were filling the treeline with fire. "Keep Up The Fire," is the 'Manchu' slogan. No targets necessary. We had no clue what happened.

Just as sharp as it started, it ceases. We listen; we hear ourselves. We look; we see the night, the slightly brighter horizon above the trees. I don't like our position so much now. What has happened? Our radio operator is whispering a situation report to his contact at the CP. We are OK; my platoon leader jumps in the hole with us. They want me at the CP, in the middle. Medics to the CP. I'd like to stay in this spot, but off I crawl; it is not far, if no one shoots me.

Thankfully, my best buddy Tommy is there. He is the second platoon medic, and the greatest guy in any kind of mess. He stopped carrying his M-16, to be able to run quicker! So tremendous and dedicated. Sadly, he has been working on Beckford. Beckford got hit! Tommy has done a great job on a serious set of wounds. He has applied pressure dressings to three spots, on the torso, I am thinking the worst, I always did, think the worst. All this patch work and moving the guy to the CP, in about a minute; man, Tommy is awesome. So, why call me? Beckford is deadly silent!

Tommy needs to start an Intravenous line. We carry fluids to bolster troops with blood loss. This is my thing; I am the needle guy - a NYC joke. I want to help; Tommy and Beckford need me. I am so scared to be in the middle of our position, and shining enough light to find veins to tap. Things get worse, as the skin is so dark and the light so bad. His veins are too deep and flattened to see, at all, and the blood loss has reduced any pressure to assist them. We are using cigarette lighters to cast our beam.

To be blunt, this is failing, and we are desperate. I have an idea to move up the arm, almost to the neck. This being something that is field expedient, to say the least. Remember that there are three entries to the torso, and dressed as well as can be. This fellow has been bleeding, five plus minutes. I have in mind to try the pulse point on the left side. Frantic, I place my hand to the back of Beckford's head, to get a better opening for my try.

My hand encounters another wound. One so very severe, that I know my man is gone. His quiet is now, my quiet. This is a man I have known alive, and that is, no longer true. I am undone, I cannot make excuse. So unnerved am I, that I virtually flee the scene. Apologizing to Tommy, that I have been no help with the I.V. line, while he is dressing the head wound, neither of us are saying the rest. They are getting an update on the Medi-Vac.

Back to my hole, I scuttle. My boys want to know, and who the hell wouldn't; nobody tells you anything, "What's up?" I told them Beckford was dead. Jeez, that was so wrong! My Platoon leader just about smacked me. My control was shot, but I knew better than to ever say, that! The guy got shot at least four times, probably at close range. No matter what I knew, the other guys were not supposed hear that. Worse yet, the chopper was pulling into this, maybe still HOT, LZ to evacuate this wounded troop. My silence now, put them at risk, as well. Not that anyone would stop trying to assist Beckford . . . and I began a process of denial, telling myself that I was wrong, incorrect, hysterical. A new story had begun. The chopper and Beckford left, without incident that night. Myself, no; he didn't leave me.

The rest took forty years to appear.

Medic Chapter Twelve: Beckford Revisited

Not Forgone, just Conclusion. The Quiet of Beckford.

Back to Cambodia, 1970 - from years, 2012, 13, & 14

Now that story is true, Heroic efforts from my fellow medic had been applied to our departed soldier. I never told him about the horrible landing my hand had made, that night. I never told him or anyone, except those two grunts in my Hole, that I was convinced of Beckford's death before the chopper landed. Never made any excuse for my weak behavior, to my platoon, or even the two in my Hole that night. Half of them thought I was crazy, anyway. Truly, my shock overwhelmed all shame. I forgave myself, it was just too much for me, even though I was a pretty hard guy by the tail end of Cambodia. One more thing, I was beginning to doubt my recollections. Enough about me.

2012, home, family, healthy, just fine, no one ever calls me DOC'.

Now you know, that all those who perished in Nam are, UPON the WALL, more than 58,000. Going there is something I have never done. Viet Nam is one year of my life, more than forty years ago. It is not forgotten or denied, just one year, of sixty-two.

On a walk with my wife, at Juniper Park, we encountered what is a mobile, miniature WALL. Very authentic and official in every way, It included the list of membership, so to speak. For reasons of respect, I sought the name of PFC Beckford. His name is not there, not upon the wall, not dead, how can he be dead, if he is not on the WALL.

He survived, no thanks to me. So glad to be wrong, yet still suspicious, in a whole new way.

I know what I know! How in this line of thought, can I dismiss this ? I could not. I now held more than confusion. Over the years, I had been contacted by one SGT from my platoon. He had sent me photos of my days, as his medic. He had gone home before my Cambodia trip. I had not ever tried to contact anyone but...there was another person who would know, for sure, about this mystery--my platoon leader. I knew he was from Pennsylvania, and began looking to contact him. He was the kind of fellow you would want for a platoon leader, friend, or brother. I would have liked to speak to him, any way. This locating took some time, mostly procrastination. As an aside, the idea of reminiscing about war days sickens me. I was drafted, never wanted to be there, and have little fondness for Army life. Further complicating this contacting of my lieutenant was his last mission. To be brief, he volunteered to go out with Recon, and got hurt. Bad. He was 'In Country', hospitalized, and I never went to see him. Because, I was angry at him. Not that he knew;...he probably did, as I told anyone who would listen, how damn mad I was at him. Also, he might be completely screwed up. You know how nutty Viet-Vets are!

2014, I called, and spoke to the guy, we called Fireball, on the phone. He sounded so much the same, and it moved me, greatly, to feel close to him again. Believe me, he was a great platoon leader and friend to me. Still mad at him for volunteering.

Anyway, he filled me in on Beckford. It was him that crawled with me, back and forth, to the CP, the night Beckford got hit. Well aware of the struggles we faced helping Beckford , HE, had been the one suppling the meager light. He remembered me trying to wipe all the blood from my hands, on the crawl back to our hole. Lastly, he knew that Beckford had died, that night. He held the details lacking in my noodle head, including the actual spelling, of our lost brother's name.

His Name is there, always was. Sometimes visited by Tommy and "Fireball" and now , , , me.

[Editor's note: For reasons of privacy, we have not used "Beckford's" real name. But I can verify this story is true because I have seen the official report of his death.]

Medic Chapter Thirteen: Good Morning Cambodia

Good Morning for a Minute, Cambodia, 1970 and very near the End of Cambodia.

I am feeling almost giddy, after yesterday's debacle at the Big Bunker Complex. We almost bit it there, for sure, and just being here, this morning, seems like a good deal. I am pulling the last watch, the last hour of watch, before the whole quiet Company of Infantry will rise at 7 A.M. or a little after sunrise. The orders of the day are not yet given. The events of yesterday were pretty immense and we will probably reenter the forested North Flank to follow up in the area of those 200 bunkers, after the Brass decide how to make it more dangerous. Maybe they will send somebody else after our heroic efforts.   Or, maybe the place was no problem now, abandoned and scouted after we blundered into it and ruined a lovely walk. Sure, today was going to go good, we deserved a break.

The overnight weather was so nice and dry, full moon and few bugs; we all had Hot Food choppered in, too, so we slept soundly. Alpha Company of the Manchus parked here next to a big paddy dike, in a dry and unplanted rice field, near the same woodline that we exited last evening. These are wide open spaces, cut into almost right angles, with expansive views of the woodlines to the East and South.   We have ideal cover from the West and to the North, hundreds of yards of open field. We are about as safe as we can be during an invasion of a country.

The sky is beginning to lighten, as I peer over the dirt and across the low scrub to the woodline, on the East. This is quite unusual, I have all the scanning opportunities in the world. My gaze is more of a pastime, than a lookout. Along the line of us, each platoon is running a watch; the other two guys are now visible to me, on my right. Each is about 30 yards from the other, and we are mostly facing the far woodline, which is, at least, 100 meters away. I am always serious about my watch, always, I've seen too many guys nod off. Have woken up, in the damn morning, in the freakin' jungle, without pulling my hour, because guys, simply feel asleep with the watch in their hands. AaK!   So, I see something, the thing you would expect to NEVER see.

Little green men, walking North, inside the far woodline to the East. Really shocked at this, I squint hard, as a third little NVA emerges, in and out of sight, heading North. Hey! That's where that Big Bunker Complex from yesterday sits. These poor clods must not know we popped it, but good. They are strolling home, I guess. My work is quickly done, as I rouse my platoon, in only a few seconds dozens of grunts are on the slant of the dike, ready to fire. By this time, there were half a dozen visible targets, just at the fringe of the woods. There was a slight delay, while the Company Commander gets a peek, and I turned away, then everyone starts shooting at about the same time. This seemed a bit like a Civil War type fusillade, such "ready, aim , fire" scenarios are the dream of combat. The reality is very little eyeballing, and lots of aimless firing down range. Personally, it revolted me; the dinks were acting like half wits. It almost made me feel sorry for them. My weapon never moved. In a brief time, they ceased firing and began to plan a move across the field, to examine the results. There was little enthusiasm for this chore, and for sure, I wasn't going.

Second Platoon went on the sweep, with one squad each from first and third. They were reluctant because of the wide open area. My whole Company was in the "survive this" mode, but we couldn't get out of this. The file spread out , North/ South, and moved quickly. The crossing was unopposed and they entered the forest upright; things were quiet. The whole bunch, more than 40 guys disappeared into the trees silently; that is how they came back.

They found: Not a Thing. Nothing to show and Nothing to Tell. The Brass circling above in Loach Choppers wanted a body count and they were not going to get... anything. Oh, man, we were sure going back to those Bunkers today.

Medic Chapter Fourteen: Boom and BOO-om

End of the Incursion, 1970 May, or maybe April, we've been out so long.

We are back at Company size, securing an LZ, for what is promised to be an extraction.

In other words, we are hanging around, about ninety of us, Alpha Company, out in the Cambodian jungle, next to a huge clearing that will soon be used for a Helicopter Landing Zone. The Invasion of Cambodia is over; we are going back to Viet Nam ...Yay. That really sounds silly, but we never hit the shit like this in Nam; Cambodia was a bitchin' time.

There is some delay about the Mechanized units pulling out, so we squat in the bush and eat.

Shocking and popping, we take fire from the distant woodline. Unusual in every way. One, the Gooks are not crazy attackers like this, and Two, the fire is from a heavy weapon, I think it is a 51, a freakin' 51, the NVA equivalent of our 50 Caliber Machine gun. An awesome weapon, the thing bangs out slugs, like the size of your finger. One inbeds itself in the ground next to me. The odd thump made me look, and the thing was exposed there. I picked it up, it burned my fingers, what a moron. As is the way here, the firing died down quickly. Hit and run, over and over, is the NVA strategy, if they have one, after the shake up we gave them.

So unexpected is this event, that the Infantry Commander has already left, on the first Chopper out, not to say he has split on us, NO. The Mechanized tracks and heavy weapons are on, down the road, as well. My Lieutenant is the senior guy here. We have zero interest in crossing the 300 meters to the other woodline to sweep. The whole thing is a little puzzling.

We can hardly ask the rest of the Choppers, en route, to hit this LZ; if we do not clear it, but if that 51' is camping out waiting, well, that would be bad for Choppers.

But wait, here come the heroes of our story !

During our 45 days, as invaders, we have had lots of weapons support; some of the best from Air Force Fighter Jets. The close contact between us has been great for us, because they "bring the smoke", man. They do that If you put them on a target! they work out like wolves at a kill. A few times we really needed them; but mostly, they just iced our already baked cake. They were all, gung ho as hell, and enjoyed talking to field troops, a lot. My Lt. felt very close to them. Best of all, a pair of jockeys we had worked with were in support today. They actually contacted us, and asked for coordinates. Excellent as these guys were, their big quirk was...they always...wanted reports on all of their damage and body counts. This was a running joke between us. They would be foaming at the mouth, after completing their runs, and we always told them we had not noticed much of anything. Of course , nothing could be farther from the truth. We loved them, and the damage, noise, fire, and general hell that they brought. Jet support always held us rapt.

We quickly set them on the far target, and settled back against our own stand of trees to observe the party. They worked out like they knew the Cambodian Party was over, because they never would get action like this again, and they knew that, too. A great show for us. They chatted up the Lt. immediately after, and in the spirit of the moment, wanted a final report. We laughingly told them, once again, that we were unimpressed. The banter was ridiculous, nobody could have more fun. The entire opposite woodline was crispy, Splinter world.

Myself and my guys were pretty sure we had heard the last of our Pilots, and were saddling up to get extracted. Lt. let us know six birds were inbound, less than twenty minutes and we would be out. Relaxed and calm, we stood, mostly facing the LZ, with the treeline to our backs when......WHAM, WHAM, we were knocked to the floor from behind. Before we could even realize anything, we heard our Jet Jockeys, howling on the radio !!

They had sonic boomed us to the ground, coming in from our backs, above the trees at about 100 feet, and a thousand miles an hour. Thanks guys and, YOU WON.

Medic Chapter Fifteen: Good Choice

1970, Tay Ninh, RVN, Platoon Leader Replaced.

I might as well tell you about Remulak, he will never know, anyway.

Why, in the hell, are we getting a new platoon leader, Now ? After Lt. Pytash, our 3-6, our own - Fireball, got off line, it is an awful question. No Officer was going to be any genuine use to us, now. We have not had any regular grunt replacements for two months. Anybody who left, was just subtracted; the platoon was only 20 guys, including me. Everyone has been jungled', for five months minimum. The last grunt moved in was from another Unit, transferred after fighting with his squad leader. Now, we are faced with an absolutely brand new Lieutenant, named Remulak. Here he is:

His feet will not line up; they wobble. He sometimes seems to be suspended from strings. If he could just straighten his stick-like legs, he would not look like he is ready to jump forward. From the knees up, the forward lean makes you think the earth is not turning fast enough. The chest, precedes the waist, the head tipping closer to you, constantly. You felt an urge to back up. The physique was quite similar to the emaciated grunts of our clan, except for the sinewy muscles grown by the months of boonie life. In short, Lt. Remulak looked wimpy, in his new boots and brand new, butter bar lapel insignia.

What had brought this fellow here was of no importance. As an Officer, his immediate job was taking our Ambush Patrol, Out. Choice does not exist. The Company Commander is a West Pointer who hates me. He will usually, either avoid me, or give me a look of disgust. Now, I see he is taking a different view. On the way out of the FireBase, he is giving me the "Take care of your Guys" gaze. We are on the same team for once. My squad leaders are guiding our FNG at every step. It is an interesting dance of having to steer, while distracting the driver. I think, quickly, of my first stroll outside the wire at FB Rhode Island. My mind was enfeebled, to say the least, and my tiny role as Medic did not come close to what Remulak was facing as a Infantry Platoon Leader on Ambush Patrol. Glancing at him, quickly showed his steps were a lot like my initial tiptoes. He peered at his wobbly steps, then popped his noodle head up, to scan in every direction. Meanwhile, he spoke into the radio and tried to look like an Infantryman. I imagined his mind has just about blinded him, by now.

We went to a set up, that Tyrod and Willis had scoped. Soon as we dropped our Rucksacks, the orders started coming out of Remulak. The guys, went about their

100

business, as Sgt. Piggott and Willis explained why we did not do any of the things ordered. It was a bit tense and the night fell on a well-set bush with a potential problem. How would our leader react in the morning?

The cool and dry morning was more peaceful, than the night. Our first business of the day was picking out new ambush sites; we were always prepared to move, or moving. Sometimes, we stuck with Platoon size sets; other times, we split into three squad size bushes. That might be just eight guys, but those were the best way to go. There would always be a few places scouted and ready. Anybody in our Platoon could pick a good bush; I was obsessed with this activity. The grunts almost never let me scope out new spots, but they dreaded my opinion if it was bad. This day, Remulak went to pick an area to bush with Willis, and could not be steered to any sensible choice. It was pretty bad stuff according to Willis. In an attempt to dodge this blunder, Piggott and Tyrod went scouting and found two excellent places. We were prepared for real trouble, if the Platoon remained intact and moved to a single bush. The day was steamy and by dusk, we were sweating more than the heat.

Our Company Commander said, ONE BUSH, heavy enemy presence. That, of course was Army Bull, but our deal was done. The Squad Leaders chatted in near silence, before we moved. The file of twenty saddled up and crept slowly to our next ambush site. On arrival, one look told me that Willis had never seen this place before! This was way too good; Tyrod and Piggott picked it , for sure. I was already happy when Remulak said to me, "Pretty good site, huh Doc".

"Yes, 3-6, you did a great job." He looked so proud.

Chapter Sixteen: R&R Questions

1970, R and R is a Question ?

While you serve your tour here in Viet Nam, time is of the essence. After a few months, you know two things about time: How much you got "In Country" and how many days left.

You might know another thing: how long until you can get an R and R. Rest and Recuperation. Recovery leave time, spent in a number of exotic locations, which are NOT Nam'.

Australia, Taiwan, Thailand, there were a few stupendous choices where you might get to spend a week.

Most, if not all troops dreamed of doing these trips and the simple pleasures of Bacchus that were associated. Bangkok was a favorite, BANGKOK! They weren't Library card expeditions.

During my time in the field, around my fifth month, a friend from childhood sent me a letter asking me to meet him at Vung Tau, a beach area up North, for the Weekend. He had enlisted in the Marines and was operating heavy equipment, like a regular job, around Da Nang. This revealed a few things to me. One, I didn't get the Weekends Off and Two, I didn't know what day of the week it was!

The Damn Gooks didn't take the weekends off, you believe those bastards? The idea of my Gung Ho Jackass buddy hanging around on a bulldozer and drinking his tour away made me really pissed off. I wrote a polite RSVP, of course, including my intention to punch his face when I saw him next. My job as a platoon medic has kept me in the field, humping my ruck and aide bag, almost constantly. My Unit, The Manchus are a Jungle dwelling species, I guess. My Company is out at Tay Ninh when we do get a day or two off. They have buildings, so it isn't a jungle. It is our rear area since we got kicked out of Cu Chi, the bigger base nearer the Saigon area. The bunkers at Tay Ninh are old and High and full of rats, but not as much as Cu Chi. We liked it fine, even though being so close to the Airstrip/ Chopper pad is probably dangerous. But we are in the rear, compared to the Dirt of Firebases and the Canopy of the field. We got our breaks, called Stand Downs, at the whim of somebody we never saw or even heard of. Whoever made up the missions we got, was like Oz behind the curtain. He cranked away at the levers making choppers and ammo. and C-Rations appear. He had plans and we were his operatives, his pawns. We were stuck.

Now, being a medic in an Infantry Platoon is a lonely occupation. You get a little caught up in the war sometimes. You begin to believe your press clippings; you are important, they tell you so! My guys were always questioning me about my commitment to get killed saving them. No answer ever lasted because every day was a new death haunting us. They knew after Cambodia what to expect: the worst soldier and the most willing friend if you had trouble. Hating the Nam' was no excuse for medics, in fact no excuses were accepted.

As my friends requested their choice of dates and destinations for R and R, I hesitated. Our Battalion Doctor had assured us that replacements were generally expected for Platoon medics at about six months in the field. The theory here was that the damn job was so dangerous, and there was work in many areas, in the rear, for Medical Personnel. So, I could just wait until that time, and avoid the unpleasant idea of sending my Platoon out...without a medic. I should never have given my mind over to this idea of actually "being" Doc Schneider. Resistance was impossible because of the men who depended on you to "be" Doc'; you are Doc'.

I waited, and as I did another thought grew. A superstitious idea, with bases deep in the brain. Based in the place that was beginning to allow me to think of surviving, the place that starts to feel the routines and actions of your daily existence are building a strength and safe haven and that any change is poisonous. Not just for you, but your whole lucky charm existence. The thought of taking a trip to a clean and safe place became a strictly forbidden act, or more like a fate clinching error, the equivalent of turning around in a horror film. My return would unleash the Wrath of Nam' and this I believed. My actions carried everyone's fate. I had mixed the Kool-Aid in the Aide Bag and injected it. Thoughts became important causes of events. Yup. Then, as often happens in my stories, things got worse.

As my six months In Country came up, I realized that the replacements were not showing up. The 25th Infantry was rumored to be pulling out of Nam' and my surroundings began to match my mentality. I still hadn't put in a request and my Platoon had not suffered a single fatality. The kettle of fate was very hot and tipping. There wasn't any way I was stirring it. The Army was going a bit loco in the area. We still worked free fire zones in the jungle and came to Tay Ninh for Standdowns, but more often than not, bad things happened. People began to believe that each foray into jungleland was the last. Short timers were no different than any one else. Everyone was in a 'get through the day' mode. The time passed and eventually I never did get an R and R, and I got crazier and bolder. After nine months, all in the field with the same Lucky Platoon and basically the same guys, we came to our last mission together. The whole damn 25th Infantry was being reassigned.   Every troop would be reassigned elsewhere.   Many would never go outside the wire again.   The deeply hated "REMF" who called the shots was giving us one last chance to be killed here, and I could not stand it. As the Company Commander, a West Pointer and my Arch Enemy, was giving the "OP. Orders," I yelled a few things at him. He went ahead and yelled back, as if I were somebody to be addressed.   He was probably going a bit nuts himself.   The Battalion had just experienced a Fragging and people were up tight as hell.   We exchanged insults and he told me, I was not fit to be in the field with his Company, and kicked me out. I was "Ruining the War" again. My Platoon went out without a medic. I survived, because I was sure to be killed, if I went.   My Platoon came out OK, too, only because I hadn't broken the deal.

Rest and Recuperate? I didn't want them to go without me.

How did they make me so crazy ?

Medic Chapter Seventeen: Stopped in my Tracks

September, 1970. Been Third Platoon Medic for almost Nine Months.

I'm sick of this mission. We moved into an area where the whole Company has been assigned to work with Mechanized Units. We choppered over here from a nice jungle, where we were hiding, and having cocoa. Squad size ambush is our way of life now, and it works fine, for the experienced troops, in my Platoon. Almost every one has been "In Country" since before Cambodia, allowing us to know the difference between playing fair, and being nothing but a target. Seven of us could prowl an area, hardly moving between set ups, picking a new ambush site and shifting when we want. My Platoon could work three at a time, which sounds dangerous, but was what we liked. There was not much contact to speak of, and most was at our discretion. We worked "free fire zones" making life simple. See it. Shoot it. This is how we have spent the months of July, August, and September.

NOW, some Military mind has cooked a stew of Mech, Armor, and Infantry, to get somebody killed. We positively hate being anywhere near these targets. They could not be more out of place, or more obvious, to the other team. The troops assigned to Mech Units relied on fire power, for everything. What else could they do? The noise and smell of them made hiding impossible! For sure, they brought big smoke, when the weapons opened up! Ordinance down range, until the actual appearance of the field of fire changed. They knocked down trees, as easy as people. Bravo!, meaning Hooray, not the Company. We would be standing around, next to these behemoths, before, during , and after they would get ambushed, crap, crapo.

It was good to see some of the friends from the other Platoons, especially my boy Tommy, the second Platoon medic. Just a great little red headed guy, from Ukiah, California. Brave and strong, he was everything I had turned out not to be. He was golden for real, his attitude was like Mickey Rooney in Nam. Always smiling and positive. I was nothing, but a suspect; my attitude a constant thorn in the side of every situation. I hated it, and I said so, constantly.   The way the Army tried to get us killed, all the time, was a little irritating. Everywhere we went, looked like the best place to get wiped out; my behavior was awful. Only my friends could tolerate me. I was a bad soldier, only being a medic kept the ship afloat. The commitment was still there, but even that was fading, before the weakening me. I had a notion that medics got replaced after six months in the field, which messed me up worse. Anyhow, I was cranky when we arrived.

With, my eagle eye, I estimated about twenty tracks, APC's, Armored Personnel Carriers, and some Tanks way up front. There were also some ARVN's, Army of the Republic of Viet Nam, up front, just to add a rancid spice to the mix. The whole area was rank, and loud, and choking, ohm I was real happy. The terrain was heading gradually uphill, the ground was anything but flat, having a mogul followed by a hillock, followed by a good old bumpy hump. The bouncing of the machines, as we moved out, would be comical, if they were toys. The full size APC, probably weighs 20 tons, the tanks 30. Seeing these skid and bumble, next to your tiny self is, just scary, but it does distract you, from thoughts of getting shot.

You also get the bugs and dirt they kick up, so there's that.

The whole column moves out to the east, the lead elements are way the hell in the mist, up hill. The surroundings are devastated from the bivouac, and the passing. The gunners, sit atop their rides, like Proud Mahuts, patting their elephants; they always had a cold Coke in the other hand. To make us feel bad, I thought. The 50 Cal, and M-Sixty Guns getting an affectionate pat, all the time, like pets. We scuttle along beside, our attention on almost anything, besides the jungle of Nam'. That does not last long.

Everything stops without reason. There is some chatter on the radio, and my Lieutenant sends me forward, ASAP. I got a long slide ahead. This is an odd situation for us, so Okie and Chanon move up with me. This is what stopped us; as I pass a bunch of APC positions, there is a lone Tank.

The Huge Tracks, that move this beast, have entangled an ARVN. He is surrounded by his mates, including their medics. In the time it takes me to approach, the man is given One, Two, Three serets (single doses) of Morphine. Just as I am about to start screaming at these jackasses, they give him One more. I reel backward with the fact, they are killing him! THEY know, he is finished, and do what should be done. What I would have done, now seems foolish.

My mind is quite jumbled, I am revolted, and turn away. Once more, the reality is more than I can absorb. The grunts with me are not sure what has happened, as we return to our position. My report to the Lieutenant includes a request to see Tommy, about me being sick. I am sick. I go straight to Tommy, and tell him, "I am sick, awful sick. Tommy, you know I am sick, dust me off." There is no way he is supposed to send me to the rear: platoon medics think they run the show, they don't.

When the resupply chopper came in, I got on it. I was sick, and I told the Battalion Doctor that when I saw him. Tommy took the blame. My Company Commander was furious. We were coming to the end of me, and my time with the Infantry. I only missed one day in the field, but some of my Platoon stayed upset about it. My superhero outfit had a hole in the butt.

Within two weeks, eventful ones, the 25th Infantry would leave Nam, and all of us would be reassigned. One very broken medic would travel North, alone.

Medic Chapter Eighteen: Cu Chi Sandwich

Oct. 1970, Stand Down, Infantry Holiday from missions. Days of the week mean nothing.

I have been "in country" nine months. Most of those days and nights, in the jungle, Mostly sleeping on the ground. Mostly, humping my food in my rucksack. Mostly miserable.

Today, I am in Cu Chi, a big base camp, with a PX and a mess hall. In just a few days, the 25th Infantry is going home. Maybe one or two more missions, and we will disband. Right now, we get a break, two days of stand-down. Pretty soon I am high, drunk and high. I got a package from home. Canned baloney, I got some, fresh bread, eating my sandwich in my platoon's hooch. NICE.

Bang! One shot, we are Way in the middle of a basecamp. I'm shocked, and stoned, and angry !

I hear some voices, people are running, "Medic!" I didn't want to hear that. Not going to spoil my party, crap, I hesitate, but I go. You, have to GO. Always. They call you, "Doc".

Down the company area, I go, to the first platoon hooch. Looking inside I see this:

Some trooper is on the floor, bunch of troops around him, I haven't yet got in the circle, when I realize . . . this is a suicide attempt! One shot to the chest, with an M-16. One medic is already there and the Battalion Doctor, he has a finger stuck, directly in the wound. I am disgusted, not by the gore, but by the idea of this jackass spoiling my sandwich, which was still in my hand.

I walked away, never regretted it, either. Really, I was past caring. It was his business, anyway. OH, yes, the M-16 is an automatic weapon. It will fire five rounds in a second. Some guys said...I was wrong. Who the hell did they think I was? You can't care; I didn't! Cause I...couldn't. The guy survived, thought you might care.

Medic Chapter Nineteen: Oh, Bravo

Cu Chi, 1970, Last Days for the 25th Infantry, in Nam'

Guess I, have to tell about Bravo Company, our only Battalion Brothers during this whole stint, protecting the area, west of Saigon. Alpha and Bravo make up the 4/9 Manchu Unit, attached to the 25th. Battalions are supposed to have five Companies and Special Weapons Units. For us, the only Infantry we ever see is...Bravo. We aren't friendly; though we come and go from the same Fire Bases and Base camps. We aren't looking to socialize and the Army always keeps one of us in the boonies, mostly both. Not only, IN, the boonies but way the hell, OUT in the boonies, and for long trips, especially since we both came back from Cambodia. The Manchus are like stray dogs; keep them... out of the yard, and we know why. The discipline, the stupid, useless, discipline, we lost that loving feeling for lifer bullshit, and shaving and, like that. We are too, gruntly, and too armed and dangerous. We have become what you really want in a war, just not in your rear area, please. Anyway. . .

Bravo has had all the bad luck; we have had the good. Honestly, it is embarassing how few real casualties my Alpha Brothers have suffered. Not to say, we were unscathed; we got scathed, but Bravo lived under the Scathing machine. Sheer numbers! No, their casualties could not be expressed in numbers; there were way too many. Worse yet, the way these men perished was maddeningly accidental in almost every case. No death at war is truly an accident, but Bravo's dead seemed tragic, in the extreme. Beyond the wrenching stories, there were the men left behind, some permanently damaged from the incidents, and almost all the rest were deadly bitter. This was the Bravo we knew was with us, in the big base camp called, Cu Chi for a standdown. The fact that the Overall Unit called the 25TH INFANTRY was being sent back to Schofield Barracks in Hawaii, had little to do with the individual grunts who were here now. Almost all of us, would simply be shipped to other horrible places in Nam', with other suffering, miserable troops that we didn't know. The attitude was, mighty bad, even as we rested for three days. There was a tiny chance that we would not have any more missions, at all. The rumors were flying, The drinking was heavy and almost everyone was loaded, one way or another. I was having a very bad time with my platoon Sarge and the Company Commander, on a personal level. The hate was there, but they had enough respect to give me room. There was little sense in exploding now, we were almost finished with this chapter. More about me later, Bravo had the shacks across the road. We played some basketball, with a bunch of them and our Alpha Company West Point Commander; things were seemingly OK. The night gave time for more rest and some guys got massages, and went to the PX, in disguise. We were not supposed to be allowed in those places, because we were...scum. The fights and nuttiness, at the PX, were bad, I must admit, and we always carried our M-16's locked and loaded. That was a problem, this far in the rear. There was talk, of making us turn the guns in, which inflamed the best of the best, badly. NO GUNS !!! These, Rear Echelon, Mo, Fos, better never try to take these guns. My Companies' attitude was a real problem, in a base camp, get it, and Bravo was MUCH worse. They hated their First Sarge, and had a big problem in the evening, out in front of their quarters. Things were looking a bit unruly, and I felt bad for all concerned. The possibility that troops could get in big trouble now was disgusting. Bravo didn't need any more bad luck. The night was very peaceful, as we slept off the resting juices. The morning brought noise and raucous shouts.

The entire Bravo Company was out in the morning sun, in front of their hootches, doing PT, Physical Training, Jumping Jacks, squat thrusts, running in place, like recruits! Some of my boys were laughing, or wisecracking, from our side of the road; not me. I knew, this was real trouble; these troopers were not going to stand for this...humiliiation, no way. I could not imagine that their Company Commander would be allowing it, but that damn Top Sarge was leading the exercise for all to see. Without any more to see, I went for a walk behind the Company area and worried. My first worry was someone doing that, to me. My pride would have literally cracked; the degradation was supreme. We are Field Troops, not trainees. We kill people for you, we get killed for you, leeches suck our blood, our friends Die. You better have... some kind of respect . After my selfish thoughts, my mind became deadly serious, The deed was done, and the consequences would surely be, on the way. Sometimes, my Medic Mojo let me intrude in matters. This was not one of that type, at all. This knowledge made me start drinking; the drinking made me belligerent. My friends made me lie down, and the Explosion, made me awake.

Late night, in Viet Nam, noise from just so far, noise from just one source, noise that brought news, and finality. Oh, Bravo. Oh so sad a place and time.

Medic Chapter Twenty: Chopper Pilot

November, 1970, traveling from Da nang to Qui Nhon. Private Schneider E-2

MOS 91-Bravo, Army medical corpsman.

Just finished up nine months as a platoon medic, with the 25th infantry. They sent the 25th back home, without me. Got sent to Da Nang for reassignment, wasted time traveling up there from Cu Chi. Having fun hitching rides on resupply choppers and trucks. I am a little bit AWOL, as the trip was scheduled to be...one simple C-130 flight, that would have taken a few hours. Orders are becoming a bit fuzzy, because of my status as a field troop in the rear. The lifers try to act like you are still "in the army", while worried you may blow up. Acting crazy is the order of the day; discipline is nothing to laugh at. People are being killed over it.

I am going to Quin Nhon, to be further reassigned. I am going, just no rush. My tour, will be three more months. They could send me anywhere; back to the field, Lord forbid it, with the 5th Mech, on the DMZ, or hospital duty, Anything; after all, I am still in the army. That is, the part of me left, after my tour down south. The strain of this field life, has weakened me, pretty badly. I have no commitment to live or die, continue to get stoned and feel angry and estranged from reality. My attitude is impossible to deal with, since I think who the hell I am. At the same time, my actual confidence is shattered. Like quite a few troops I meet, my ability to control myself, is questionable.

Arriving at my new assignment, a Dustoff/Medivac unit, I meet the head honco. He is a CW 3, Warrant Officer, chopper pilot, working as the commanding officer of this unit. Warrant officers, who fly medical evacuation helicopters are the most revered individuals in Viet Nam, especially among Infantry Units, like the Manchus' grunts I humped with. This man has taken more risk on behalf of guys in deep trouble, than a comic book hero. Compared to my field medic status, he is...a living god. Meeting in his office for the first time, I am very humble. Oddly, he seems to feel the same way, about my Infantry gig, remarking that he understands how spent I must be. I am honored to be recognized as someone of value, though feeling , very weak.

He explains to me, the duties which are performed by his unit medics. Simply put: They get on the chopper, whenever, ride and deal with whatever fantastic danger and traumatic injuries occur each day. He tells me to take that evening to think it over, as No More line action is required of me. I have done my bit as it were, according to him. Nine months of platoon medic, is actually more than most ever do. I am given the choice to pull guard and camp duty, or take my place among those flying. This is so great, I can hardly keep from blurting out the answer. I act sober, and tell the man, goodnight. Went to my new quarters, which had a bed and sheets, and wood walls, and was actually two stories tall. I was so far in the rear!

As the evening turned to night, my broken mind was churning; my childish pride was bubbling, my traumas from the 25th, were nagging. Most of all, my respect for that pilot, was whittling away at the facade of indifference. In the morning, and it was early in the morning, I went back to the office. I looked to the face of the pilot and he knew---I began to cry, as I told him I could not do the chopper gig, that nothing was left. The call of it was wrenching the heart from me! How truly sorry I was, to deny this opportunity to go down in a blaze of heroic glory! and he Understood, perfectly.

Why? I think the call that made him a medivac chopper pilot, let him know how I felt.

Medic Chapter Twenty-One: Home Coming Chill

December 1970, Jamaica Avenue, by the elevated train. NYC

The cold seemed to rise up out of me, and into the winter sky of 110 st., through the naked branches. The trees by the "EL train" always were weak from the fight. I'd been away some time, 11 months plus, and I wasn't discharged yet.   Just back from Nam, if not back . . . closer.

I'd traveled 14,000 miles of distance easier than the walk down this block.   One full block, and I would see my home, see my Mom and Dad, little brother and sisters.   Yes, and they would see me.

People say, "every fiber of my body," when they express desire. I was torn, fiber from fiber. Each longing to be returned to this place, got struck by the me, who was different, by the other me, the one who needed to hide.

The steps, the sidewalk, the cold, and the simple task at hand; go into your own home, as someone else.   An identity thief, who now replaces the previous you. You are different, plenty different from the you they want back.

I can't come back. I am gone! It hurts to be so damaged and distant. Most of all, you want to avoid your Mom knowing her little boy, is gone. He got hurt. She suffered so much, while you were gone. Part of you knows, you will always be gone. . . and now, you go up the steps to the porch.

Things are unchanged, the McG tree is still huge, the steps and porch, are still gray painted wood.   The front door glass and vestibule are no different. Everyone looks the same. Everyone, is the same. All they wanted was to see you. Of course, you're happy to be home, but you desperately want to say, "don't look at me."

What you mean is: see the old me, the child me, the undamaged me. The me you want, not, THIS me.

Medic Chapter Twenty-Two: Tiny United

Feb. 1971 Sent to Germany

Wackenheim, Yes Wackenheim. It's a place. An Army Station in West Germany. This assignment comes my way as filler, time-killer, like packing, to complete my two year commitment, as a draftee . Been in the Army, 18 months. Time enough to get trained, shipped to Nam, and come back home. One month at home on leave, and five more, "Army" months to kill. I, am a miserable soldier, never was any good, Worse now, I am truly damaged emotionally. Don't start catching feelings, for me yet, the party isn't over.

The transition from leave, to Over seas flight, to base in Germany, is one crummy drudge. The Barracks areas that hold you on travel orders are called 'Transit Companies'; they are an easy place to abuse the Army. Nobody knows anybody, or where they are going. Deadbeat, Awol, missing and hiding troops, often frequent these areas. Likely places to waste time. Friendly places for hobos like me.

Along with some of the sleaziest transit bums, are genuine U.S, soldiers. They are on a military mission, often horrified at the random nature of these companies. I have my orders to report to the Medical Battalion, attached to the Airborne unit, at Lee Barracks. Sounds quite awful good odds of me being in the Frankfurt Stockade, within the week. My respect level is frighteningly low. I Salute Officers only on demand, looking for trouble. By 1971, the Army was infected by the outside world. Many winds blew through the ranks, to chill the order.

As I said, transit is cake in the Army. Airborne Units are, strack! You starch up and march tall, snap off salutes, and act macho military. Honestly, I might get killed by the troops, forget the officers. I have no respect for this chicken shit, rear echelon fakery. The Nam' will do that. Still hopeful about the prospects, though feeling depressed and sick, there is a "tiny" amount of relief, and even pride in having survived Nam'. During the whole tour my opinion, regarding my " glorious service", remained the same. I didn't wanna' be there! Had I been prideful at all, I would not still be a Private First Class. Everyone coming home, was a Spec. 4 , at least one rank higher. My specialty has always been in avoiding favor. Very prideful of the level of frustration and anger produced among my superiors. Feel strongly, that even as a draftee, I have become a major nuisance.

Far as this Germany trip goes, I can take it or leave it. Not as full of resentment as might be expected. Hating the Army doesn't qualify you for any other life. Outside of this spiteful waste of time, my time was wasted. Not one meaningful aspect was left, of my existence. So, you're here now dopey, why quit ?

Traveling by truck to Frankfurt, and North toward the city of Mainz, is no misery...it's pleasant really. There are no duties, just travel orders. Wish I knew more, so as to wander for a few days. Pitifully, there is not the strength for any antics. "Played Out" returnee, resisting the stigma of my identity, and any other identity, as well. Damaged, and pretending to be in control. Man! my stupid ass woulda' flew, all over that place before. Now, I act like a mope, sulk, it ain't like me.

Catch a ride for the final leg to Wackenheim with a "deuce and a half" trucker convoy. Huge, Diesel, troop trucks, 6 of em', filled with supplies and a few soldiers. My ride splits off from the pack, further North for the last bit. Off the highway, through the little town and upward, in the middle of farms and vineyards and ancient homes. UP - Up to Wackenheim!

This is my assignment. Ever so cheerfully, the post of the 8th Medical Battalion is nowhere near that goddam Airborne dump. Wackenheim is a hilltop collection of cardboard box-looking, block buildings, behind a weak and wimpy front gate arch. I arrive with a resupply truck, the best way to travel, if you ask me. Spent plenty of time bouncing around on resupply choppers in Nam, and these truckers here are no different. Been back from Nam about 40 days. My previous drug problems are mostly gone. Mostly. We Blow right through the check at the gate. Hello, Wackenheim. The company is up the hill to the right, the Battalion HQ, is first on the left. Gotta' stop in with my orders. See the Bird Colonel, get the speech; oddly he's asking if I'd like to be " Airborne"; they need jump qualified medics. "Gumballs , Sir. No training for me, back from Nam, you know." Shockingly, he says, they will strap me up and let me take a qualifying jump, right away, screw the training! Crap! as bad a soldier as I am, that is, NOT RIGHT! Guys knock themselves out to become "Airborne", it's a big, goddam' deal. The stateside training at Fort Benning is an ass kicker. Sheesh, this place is extremely odd. No Thanks, Sir, I want to yell at him. Some things are serious; this clerky Colonel guy is just filling dance cards. Maybe the Army actually "got" part of my brain! I was so furious about this, why should I care? Shows how you still care, even when you can't care. Confused me, bad. Sent up the hill with little more than instuctions to "Go see Weidenhoffer", the Top Sarge of Barracks One. In Wackenheim style, Barracks One was the Last One. Top of the Hill.

Now, most of my drug problems from Nam, were pretty far behind me. Did a bunch of drinking on leave, and smoked some. I meet some troops, by the jeep drivers, outside the HQ, nice guys, they are obviously, "heads". Everyone is adding tiny touchs to the Uniform, such as neckpieces or rope figures to undermine the uniformity and show their colors. They can give me a ride up the hill, and we can stop, at their shack, Barracks Two. Cool with me, never any rush for me, never. Laughingly, these guys are hash smokers. OK by me! but I have never seen this kind of hash smoking, in my life. They mix tobacco and hash, half and half, and fill a pipe. A Meerscham bowl, and we smoke two! This is like, too much, like an ounce of hash, jeez these guys smoke, Way too much, 8th Medical Battalion. Hash! My Lord, they smoke so much! Way too much.

Go straight, haha, to the company office of my ambulance platoon. Meet Sergeant Weidenhoffer, he seems nice, for real.

I can't even read the material given me by the First Sergeant, so I decide to pretend to read for about the time it should take. Only, I have no sense of time, man, they smoke too much hash !

Because, I think because, of my played out appearance and my status as "back from Nam" the Top, ships me off to my Quarters. This is the beginning of six months of favoritism and special treatment. I am essentially...the only Nam Vet in the company. It helps. But even this, will not make my military life smooth.

My quarters are up a central staircase of a two story rectangle shaped building. From there we turn left, and then, around to my corridor. Each room of the place is big enough for dozens of bunks and there are six divisions on this level. The place, is half empty and looks spacious, if not lonely. Great by me, crowded barracks are violent barracks.

It is apparent, my arrival is expected; the corner bunk---farthest from the door is open for me. Obviously, the best location, this seems the second indication of the favoritism headed my way. The Nam Vet, the boiling, invincible, frightening psycho, was announced, prior to arrival! In fact, most of the troops here came straight from training stateside, I was about the only one, with any experience , among the ranks. Had I agreed to stay in Nam' two months longer, this torture could have been avoided. Many did just that, and were discharged early. The choice was not really there for me. No Way.

Though the conditions of these bunks and blankets and clothes were no large burden, they all seemed to exert a weight, upon me. Though my roommates were not so awful, they could not always be what could help me. Misery loves company, we were those two things, and man they smoke too much!

Attitude problems, sad really, almost anyone could cruise these six months, even enjoy them. The surrounding area was very beautiful, and the work was...non-existent. Some of the people were gold, like anywhere; the guys make the place. Almost anyone could find a little niche to inhabit.

Almost anyone, but I am, SO different.
The guys in my room, are all hash smokers; they drink too. Wine and Coke mix. Never seen this before either, White wine and Coca Cola, half and half, back in the bottles. You pretty much, cannot taste the wine, and get stupid drunk, accidentally. Then, you smoke a few bowls of hash in the "cooker", our big Meerschaum pipe.

Our little group is, misfit toys. Describing their various, non Army qualities might shock many, but remember this was a draft induced flame, burning the barracks. Of course, we had a girlie troop, so effeminate that he was almost, a real girl. A great guy as well, most of us loved our girl.

We had the guy who is way too childish to be in the Army guy. We had the 'stoner moving to Bangkok' guy, the trying-to-complete-his-time guy, the scared of getting in trouble guy, and Strausse.

This poor Strausse had never been out of his small town in the mid-west. He had never been around anybody different, and never met a black man, person to person, in his life. A knack for misstepping with the "brothers", had him under some evil pressure. Not entirely innocent, he had become a target, and was way unable to manage at all.

The reason the U.S Army is here, to protect West Germany from Soviet invasion, does not come up much here, in Wackenheim, We just run the engines on "cracker box" ambulances and have two formations a day. If combat occurs, we will be rapidly defeated. The real Army base, at Lee Barracks is, way more serious. Wherever they go, and they, ARE AIRBORNE, we go.

We, are attached to them. Like, if they make a practice jump, we watch from the fields below and hopefully, that is all. That has been the only real work of this group for many years. Jump coverage is mostly a pleasant afternoon, ruined by some injured guys, in Cochrane boots. Occasionally, well. . . !

Germans think of us as an occupation force. Pretty sure most have nothing but hate for us. Some of this hate is caused by the behavior of the troops, who periodically run amok in towns throughout Europe. There is also some racism in Germany as well, shocking.

No matter, we are pretty isolated, up here in Wackenheim. We're at the top of a long series of hills, above the towns of Ingleheim and Finthen, looking down on the Rhine River and across to the Taunus Mountains. It is a beautiful countryside, which I can appreciate for providing many places to be alone. I do feel alienated enough to leave everyone behind, at times. Not for big thinking, more to be in a vacuum.

I have a guitar, friends, enemies, problems; it is social engineering, maybe easier for me than most. The Army crap is low-key, still it is a struggle for me. I'm undisciplined from Nam', can't keep up my appearance, fail inspections, can't fold my socks and belts in my little foot locker. Depressed and angry. It must be getting very difficult for the lifers to deal with me, especially in the way it affects other untainted troops. Some of these lifers, slang for Army regulars, were beginning to develop a genuine hatred and resentment, toward me. My influence on the company, as a whole, was not conducive to discipline. Often high and surly, my indifference led lesser knuckleheads to try their luck. For a while, time passed, but the Army of 1971, had many ways to leave you, upended. Now To, TINY

Black Militants, Army style; Germany had plenty. Add pothead radicals and disgruntled G.I.'s, and you have a potent mix. The young men in this dump are mostly playing games with the Army, and each other. To say it again, the racism was there. For instance, my room was all white guys, and we had "StrausseRace" trouble, Not just by reputation, he was involved in some hostility, before my arrival. My presence quelled a bit of his stormy life, and my life in NYC, gave me a little respect, in both camps . Prior to my arrival, literal space invaders would show up, to harass this guy. Mostly directed at him, this type of gangup shit wasn't making any whiteboys too friendly, either!

The Post is relaxed , the discipline weak . Time goes by, fences are mending. Some are content , others await, in anticipation.

The 8th Medical Battalion is chock full of crummy soldiers. In sum, they aren't much. They treat me, like something special. I am a "Viet Nam Veteran", something they hope never to be, and stil, probably, want to be, in a way they will never shake. Everything is about Nam', all over America's mind, it circles. Protest, Massacre, the image of the mad, invincible , boiling veteran! These lucky jerks here got shipped to Germany; reasons unknown to me spared them...the Asian Vacation.

Plenty of race tension spices up the barracks. Some days it seems the central issue. Most of the white troops have never interacted with black people. I imagine the reverse is true. The black trooper, is almost lockstep militant. They come from everywhere. Peer pressure to enter this, new dead end of militancy, is intense. It is just easier, to wear the Militant vogue, so they do. I have plenty of pretenses, too. I am a Radical, Subversive, Lethal friend of the Militant. Sabotage, resist, and pound out the dap' with my brothers. Wish, in truth, to be somewhere else, and do not care about anybody, but myself. It's a grind, relieved by some genuinely friendly and helpful buddies, believe me, the help was needed.

Fraternizing is frowned upon, by the "blackest of the black" separatists; these are made up of genuine idealists, wanna' be gangsters, and outright fakers. As always, the strongest of individuals cannot be controlled, by this weak mentality. Besides, there are unifying forces at work. Many of the troops hate the Army, above any division.

There are also people like Lee; everyone calls him "Reverend Lee". HE, and his friend Dog are the kind of guys who own themselves, and all around them. If you are not on their team, where the hell are you ? Not racist at all, above the dirt, leaders, friends. There are people like Wieber and Danny, that make the day laugh at itself. There are many, just caught between, in time and place. As I said, mostly anyone could do this little bit, but for me. . . This is like a penance, the time passes, as I maintain my poses. Very tough to tolerate some of the jerks caught up here. There are white boys who are full of race trouble, worse than Strausse. This forces real tension, on everyone. The lifers, don't come near this issue, except for one thing ...TINY.

Tiny has been away in Frankfurt Stockade, for hitting Thomkins and breaking his jaw. Thompkins is the Anti-Christ. His room is the mirror image of mine, on the flip side of the stairway. He cares only for drug money, town hookers, and himself. Obnoxious to the point of comedy, he thinks the hookers love him, cause he is such a man! It is no mystery why Tiny hit him, more like, why NOT? Tiny is going to be a fearsome presence, many men here are just plain...scared. I should really let you know how you might make Tiny mad. You might be: too Black, too White, or, also, you might be, not black or white enough. Do not blame Tiny; these are real/imaginary categories. Frighteningly, I may qualify for ALL !

HE, will be back soon, and Thompkins is still here! Described to me as a racial incident, I know it involved hash, and maybe more. Thompkins is a big boy, but, he wants no more of Tiny. His crew is mighty scarce, since the assault. That does not mean, they are not here. I do not have anything to do with them. White weasels, not worth the time.

My current position, King of the Barracks, makes this my business. My friend, Reverend Lee, King of all things black, has filled me in on this, including the race angle. He is a great friend to me. Dignified and unaffected by fakers, he seems to understand things easily, maybe his Roberta Flack album gives him powers. He is the King in my book. Not racist at all. Where such guys come from is, a mystery to me. He tells me, "Tiny will be coming to see you." Maybe he is upset that I am avoiding tension, and am, in such favor with everyone. Of course, I have some enemies, the kind who await your fall because, low is where they live.

Most young men, are just passing time. Prisoners are doing time. Army, like me in Germany, are close to prisoners. The issues of the day mean zero, but in 1971 Germany,   there was a legitimate radical culture in the barracks. Led by Black Militants and co-authored by troops alienated by U.S. policy and Vietnam. The counter culture of America penetrated well, in the minds of those sequestered far away. Much honest fervor existed. It is a Given that most low ranking draftees, just want to reach their DEROS [date of estimated return from overseas]. These concerns clashed for control, for you will not be reaching your deros while in Frankfurt Stockade -no. That is, "bad" time, not counting toward your DEROS. So express your hippie politics, gently.

For me, commitment to a group or creed meant nothing. I was proud to be accepted by anyone. As months passed, my attitude began to change, less careless, more Army, scared to get in trouble, so close to my deros. This led to my undoing, with my enemies. Pressure to display my invincible, anti-army attitude   began to mount, and now here comes Tiny, to my Quarters. To my little corner.

Although the room is large enough for ten bunks, there are only six. My friends have warned me, but they are standing back. Strausse is standing by his bunk, on my left, skittish as a buck. The dynamite is rolling, the fuse is burning.   My cartoon is getting, scary.

Tiny enters with a posse of "boo koo dap brothers", wearing black rope crosses. Half of them are from another Company. Normally, they would not stroll in on me, it just wouldn't happen.

I am sitting in my Mercedes Benz bucket seat, on the floor, it's nice. I don't get up. Tiny walks directly to me, my situation could not be weaker. If, he is bent on putting me down, I will be crushed.   For sure, no one will help me.   At least I know that his posse is full of non-factors; they know me more than four months, without incident. It suits their ganged up purposes to shut down any black/white friendships, which undermine "unity". They've had no success with my friends.

Tiny and I shake hands; he offers no dap, no brotherly love, but no hate. Hard to describe the size of Tiny, standing there, reaching down to my hand. Tiny, wants to know, if I am protecting anyone, which he knows I have been doing. I 've been like Rambo/Billy Jacking the place! Strausses' eyes are just about rolling back in his head. I already know, this is not about Strausse, or even Thompkins. This is about Tiny, Tiny wanting to DEROS. These "friends" of his, are trying to send the guy back to Frankfurt. Their 'Champ' will take the fall for these punks, except "Tiny ain't havin' that." I see it. And, I am with that. Now, we get the help we need.

My door pops open and in walks Thompkins. This Idiot probably thinking to settle all his accounts, at once. His "boys" are in, MY DOORWAY, you heard ?

The bell sounds, and I am up out of my bucket, and flying at Thompkins, grabbing him and yelling, "You can't walk on me like that, you don't know me like that. " He is too shocked to resist, as I throw him into his boys, out of the room and slam the door.

Filling my lungs, I looked at Tiny; he was laughing. I felt, a little hysterical, myself. I cracked up, too, but behind my eyes was a little burning sensation. Wieber and Danny were jumping around while I sat back down. The door opened slowly, I really did not want that. Reverend Lee poked his head in and said, "Wanna Smoke ?" Man, they smoked TOO much.

The militant side of things continued to badger me, throughout my final two months in Germany. They could see my politics were fake. As you can see, I really can fake it. My revolution would come for, only me, and that was a few odd years away.

Medic Chapter Twenty-Three: Video and Tobor

Back to Wackenheim, 1971, Germany

Our main pastimes up here on the hill are: Wine, cards , and hash. There are days when...we party a bit, and days when we get wasted, all day. Being in the Army doesn't take much time at all. A formation every morning, and the occasional detail with our Cracker Box Ambulances. Most of our time is idle and unsupervised. But, enough about the Army, this is the story called, " Captain Video and Tobor go to Frankfurt."

My good buddy, Lenny Van Dam is one hilarious Chicago comedian. He lives to laugh, and to be loaded. He cannot control his giddiness, even when sober, which he rarely is. Lifers try to get mad at him, and fail; they crack up with his sniffling chuckles. "Get back in line Troop." "Try to straighten up that gig line, Van Dam." "VAN DAM," they yell, and everybody cracks.

He, is my Main Pipe Partner, always with the Hash and the Connections. He has little sense in his head, and likes to hear my stories, listening with the eyes wide open that see, nothing. He Says, "the visions come to him" while I speak; this is why he calls me, Video. He is given to an almost catatonic state, which is why I call him, Tobor. As tiny kids, we both saw and remembered the TV show that invented the names, as well.

I have a Framus, 12 string guitar. I play Canned Heat's "On the Road Again", on the base strings, over and over. Everybody thinks that is, virtuosity. Mostly, time is just passing and that is all we want, but Lenny has a problem. Loopy, the post drug dealer is overcharging for the Hash, which is true. The damn punk is making a mint, marking up the chunks to twice the price. This really is not a problem because the stuff is still cheap compared to Stateside prices. Lenny is just pissed that Loopy won't give "us" a break. Loopy is a chicano guy named Miguel, who brags about how loopy his hash makes you. He goes to Frankfurt and buys it by the Kilo, which is either risky or terribly risky. He has told us everything about the Park there where you can find all the drugs. Lenny thinks we should just 'go down and cop' for ourselves, as if, it is a walk in the park.

Being from NYC, I knew that, copping a Kilo of hash in a big city park, was a lot more serious than my Tobor could compute. As a partner, eventually my presence would be required, so preparations were made. My long leather duster, I won it in a card game with Grublack, would help me profile, as a Rad' dealer. The word Rad', short for Comrade/ Radical, is used to describe, The local boys, or sometimes

Germans in general; it isn't a term of endearment. Without a gun, the right profile might help prevent us getting ripped off. For sure, two novice buyers with pockets full of Deutschmarks, would make a nice target. I'm often mistaken for a German National, my civilian clothes never said, Americanish. Lenny had a dark look that didn't invite any bullshit, either. Saturday morning, we went down into Finthen, got on the local trolley. We called it the Bahnstrasse, and headed for the Bahnhof, the Major Train System, into Frankfurt.

Constantly reminding Lenny about being stern, seemed to be sinking in. We rarely got high in the Outside world. The Rad' Police were trouble. In fact, the regular folks were not so G.I. friendly. Rad' boys are no joke and have little use for U.S. soldiers.

Riding the Rails in Germany is enough to keep you distracted by itself. It wasn't as if we were junkies; just looking to cop like junkies. The trip went fine and we had a lot of fun. By One O'Clock, we were entering the Main Park in Frankfurt, smoking a bowl as we walked. The place was full of the people, and their culture. The Gardens, the children, bikes, strollers, babies, and many flowers. Stands or Wooden Carts sold drinks and foods, the ideal setting for a Saturday with the Family. Europeans seem to have invented the "Park".

Of course, our attention was elsewhere. Among the people of Frankfurt, we could see lots of hippie/seedy friends. With plenty of time, we skirted the courtyards and lawns. Behind some big hedges, we popped in on two young girls, shooting up. Pretty, but craven, they were stone cold drug seekers, the type who are only interested in getting loaded . Lenny thought they were potential partners for us, in one way or another. What a rube, there existed between us, only the flimsiest of bridges. We smoked a bit with them, our own Black Hash in our Big Cooker Bowl, while they were cooking some black opium crosses. I had never seen this before, thinking they were nuts to even try that. Lenny was in love and just swooning over the two of them. Once they started, " booting the shots", we split. The time of the day was right to do business, and get back on the Bahnhof, and the hell outa here.

The Grassy Knoll, where the Hippies Ruled, was the marketplace. All business, we approached the different crews there, and opened trade talks. Tobor was sampling the various hashwares. The black hash alone would make you dopey, the red would strangle you into oblivion, and the green would keep you smoking forever, happily. I was relaxing a bit, too. If any "ripping off" was going to happen, this was not the place. Too many people of all kinds. Lenny wandered around speaking to each person he bumped into, which meant everybody. We were having a hell of an afternoon.

Around, five o'clock, my muddled mind was made up on buying a half a key of black, from a huge crew at the center of the Knoll. The stuff was legit, and the Rads' spoke English, so there was no "confusion" about terms, well, in a expert hashly way. Just gotta' scoop up Tobor and transact. By now the park was callin' us, Captain Video and Toborf, but Toborf , {what is the sense of correcting errors that make you laugh? } I was calling him Toborf by now, BUT he was not available. He was in a tiny tent with a few trippers. He was very animated, very unlike my Tobor on hash; he was spaced out, in the extreme. To say I was angry would not fill the slot; what the hell was wrong with this guy. He was gonna' get me "Radded"

I wanted to scream, VAN DAM !

Oh, but, Video, there is Such a good reason for Toborf's behavior. Toborf had decided to cop' Acid, and following what he thought was good business practice, he 'sampled a few different brands'. In fact, the dealers were a bit impatient for his decision. He had at least five hits, in his mechanism. VAN DAM

Now, all my paranoia preparations looked...sensible. With Lenny, I would have thrown down, with the Whole Knoll Crew, but with this 'fried shrimp', I had to look for an escape hatch for both of us. Plan B, Captain Video, ASAP. Using Lenny's money, 100 marks, I picked the cheapest hits. That satisfied those guys. From the Hash Cartel, I copped small, - 100 grams, This made me look small time, but I hoped we could leave without any hassles and not give away the 1000 marks in my pocket. The sun was setting, and Lenny was not up to any trip to the train. The result looked like, forcing me into a night in the park with Who Knows What /or Who. The sun goes down, as it does our Girls stroll by, and rescue us.

"For sure, For sure," this phrase is the most central part of the minimal English we exchange. Can we go out with you, from the park with you, with you? We are adopted and walk out of the park with these two junkies. Hard as I am, I kinda' believe they are on our side; they just...love...Lenny. The more spaced out he gets, the more they love him. The Train is a great distance away and my Tobor is not fit for public exposure; he gurgles, giggles, and speaks of Universes and Childhood pets. His vision is Impaired/ Enhanced. This becomes a problem that the girls notice, and we have to shut down the expedition. My mind is torn between relief that the park is behind us, and the worry that we are headed for a pre-planned gang assault.

We stand in front of an abandoned building, a big one of about six stories. Incredibly, it has an American Express sign on the facade. Our hosts are inviting us in, to their home. We have little choice, as I am guiding Tobor like a shopping cart. In and up the stairs, which smell of the fires of days past. Above the first floor, everything has been burned and hosed, smelling like basement comics and burnt hair. There is no light, other than what slithers through the empty window pockets. Our angels' lead us to their 'Queens Chamber', a dry and airy place of sanctuary. They have blankets, and water. This genuine offer of shelter, is so touching to me. Lenny slumps to the floor, as soon as we enter. I, sit and stare at the stairway, awaiting the thugs. The pair of Beautiful German Girls, lay beside Lenny and pull the covers over all three, very queitly. Alone, I feel like a proud parent, viewing beautiful children.

They have given everything to us, and asked for nothing. I, lay my head down on the concrete, in an American Express Building in Germany and sleep peacefully. VAN DAM.

Section Three   Adult Life   page#

Chapter A: Pool Game Winner

Year is, 1972. Sometimes, You Win.

I go to the bar and I drink beer. Unemployment checks, not much, but enough to prevent desperate straights. This bar is pretty action packed; friends, pot, enemies, girls. Worth the trip.

Meet some girls, they drink; they drink, uh huh.   I shoot pool for beers and I win, because I am way better than the bar level game. Spent four years in Bills', on Jamaica Avenue, playing Chicago with Fast Eddie L., for cash. Mostly the bar is an easy waste of time; nothing better to do, anyway. One day bounces into the next night.

I do see good girls in the bar, not many, but I see one, NOW. She just put a quarter up on the pool table, means she wants to play. I love the way she looks, her face is so sharp and features so clean, so defined. It is a pretty face, with a turned up nose and natural as can be.

I love that face, and the hair is spectacular, beautiful dark and long. Parted in the middle and falling across her cheeks. She is very slim, her top is black with tiny white dots. I am looking very close and this, is some good girl!

Not every pool game has to be for money, though I usually play for something. My friend Kathy tells this new girl, "This is for beers," and the reply thrills me; "If I lose I'll buy his beer." She showed a lot of heart and did not back off, at all.

Neither did I.   No one wants to be toyed with when they are serious; this player got her beating and headed for the bar. She bought and gave me that beer. By this time I was completely taken. Everything I saw and heard from her - Christine- was perfect. Seems like, she liked me, too. She left with some friends of hers, maybe a boyfriend, It didn't matter. Perfect girls almost never show up, and they never do come back, but she did!

When she did, she never really left again. I didn't have the courage then, to even hope for the best; the best...just happened. I'll tell you more, maybe another time. I'll tell you this now; the best can happen. Winner.

Chapter B: On the Value

On the Value of Her

unveiling and unfailing love.

love her meekly, her completely

me weekly, me discreetly,

her daily, her deeply

me palely, me weepy

As love can grow, it can grow slow

These are like the love I know,

loves me correctly, me intellectually

her erectly, her directly

me monthly, me generally

her gruntly, her tremendously

As love can fade, it can evade

This is a love, I'm afraid

I love her steadily, wait for her readily

she is the birth of it, and buddy she is worth it

Chapter C: Welcome Home, You Little Hero

November 1971 Welcome Home you little Hero.

With Christmas coming, and the winter peeking into NYC, my thoughts turned to money. My Unemployment check only covered my drinking, so I began seeking a job. I'd once had a position in a Wall Street firm, E.F. Hutton, before my Asian vacation. I did not feel fit enough to go over to Manhattan looking for that level stuff. In fact, my confidence was way down.

In those ancient times, Department stores were ruling the Holiday Events. They would hire extra help for the period, manual labor type workers, and I thought, maybe that could get me started toward a normal career path. So, onto the Jamaica Avenue elevated train went scruffy Mike to apply at Gertz, a major store in our area. On the Subways in N.Y., there were always a line of cardboard posters installed, along the upper sidewalls of each car. Advertisements and Public announcements from Transit, like the Miss Subway winner. One of these was about a hiring out-reach program, beseeching employers to consider the Disabled, the Ex-Offender and the Vet. I stared hard at it. Honestly, I understood it well. America had created us and they had to put us somewhere, but the insult stung. In a sense, I was a disabled ex-offender in the minds of America. My stop came up, Parsons Boulevard, and into Gertz went our job seeker.

The applications were simple and an interview was set up, immediately. As usual, Lucky Mike hit the jackpot. The fellow in charge of the whole receiving department was a High School classmate of mine; his name was Morris. He had a little office carved out of boxes and clipboards that smelled like glue. His face had changed a bit since 1967, when we graduated. The new mustache was an incomplete fuzz whisper, and his cheeks had continued their descent, bringing the upper lip along with them. He already had too much flesh on the jowls in High School, and eventually the whole thing was doomed to collapse into mush. That day was close. We were, 22 years old now. I weighed 155; on the other side of the desk, there were two of me.

I was happy to see Morris, he was not anybody special to me. It just made me comfortable in a nervous situation. After the briefest of hello chats, he began explaining the work of taking in boxes and opening them and counting things. He was really good at these tasks and each one had a skill set. As soon as I absorbed the depth of the subject, a feeling of dread set in. The thing was so simple that I feared I had missed something. My mind was wandering, that has always been a problem for me. Morris brought me back to reality by saying, "You're back from Nam, Huh?" "Yeah,

I been Back." I didn't want to talk about it with him, it was none of his business. He didn't 'know me' like that. Admittedy, I was tight about it. Then, he says, " BUT, Are you, ALL the Way Back ?" I twitched. Looking at Morris gave me lonely chill. This question was like a part of the interview. I got up and left, he may have been speaking as I did, but I don't know.

I got called to start the job the next morning. Even though it was his department, we hardly spoke again during that Christmas season, which concluded my work at Gertz. I was really bad at the Box Counting.

Chapter D: Hometowner

Outsiders 1972 Back in my Hometown, NYC

When I walk these familiar streets, there is a feeling of not belonging, of sneaking past the wooden porches and decorated windows and front yards.   The alleyways and fences push me away and the curtains are: to prevent my gaze, to be slightly moved to see my passage, or assure it more likely.

The few months since my discharge have allowed my furry appearance to approximate...regular degenerate youth.   The area of Queens where I grew up was now loaded with long hair miscreants and apprentices.   The community was never going to be comfortable with these changes, which came so quickly and against the will of our 1950's Catholic parentage.   They didn't fight the Big One to allow decadence to prevail.

When viewed from outside, I was a tall, blond fellow, who strode along with his big shoulders back and head held high.   Though nobody knows your feelings, they always seem exposed.   The unclean hangover from the Jungle Rot was still all over me.   The day light was no time for a young man to be Unemployed and Out of school, wandering the tender streets of Richmond Hill.

The trip to the Park and Pool Room, made me think too much.   During the day, I never went to the Bar, that's a rule.   I tried hard to save my unemployment check for Bar money.

Once again, Forest Park became an easy friend. Once there, you had options about choices. Yes, redundant as that sounds, you could be "what/ where" you wanted. The young had pretty much conquered the place.   The Precinct Cops stopped by, like always, but the enthusiasm wasn't there anymore.   The emergence of so many crazy kids made things a matter of priorities.   Scattered about the Parks were Crazy Gathering places, where nightly drug markets and fights made for an arrest bonanza. I certainly still feared the local Cops, who always let you know who ran the Park, but by 1972, they were backing off heavily.   The people who hung at Forest, by the Jackson Pond Area were just decent kids; there were bigger problems.

For me, lucky Mike, the place was a Haven.   There, I found an acceptance that apparently many Vets never found at all.   The opportunity to resume my childhood, really.   An interesting social revolution had begun, what can only be described as "the extended childhood."   Good thing for me, as my mentality was so stunted by the military assistance.   Along with being a lifelong diehard Parkboy, I was blessed with a crew of younger friends ready-made by my brother. His buddies, either knew me from before my service, or heard about me while I was gone. They all drank or got high, while they drank and got high, while they played ball, all day. Then, later, they did two of those things some more. Some of them did not ever get high, play ball, or do anything else, they just hung out, which was a major skill. You could do that, seemingly it was all good. Maybe they did do something else; that would be OK, if it was a secret. The attitude of acceptance was remarkable, really.

Since the area was a huge playground space, the main activities were sporty. I always played all sports, so, perfect. The younger boys and lots of great girls had a beautiful social scene carrying over from having a long acquaintance in school and neighborhood. Being a little older, by six years, kept me a bit separate on the date front here, but I was already involved that way at the Bar. When I first met these Pond People, they were about sixteen and still in High School. My 22 years made me a complete old guy. That was OK, I felt that way myself. I carried a lot of self deprecating ideas, that would set me back for a couple of years.

Interestingly, few of my original peer group were still around. Their growth had not been stunted like my own. They were grown ups, horridly, many had missed the revolution altogether. In this short period of 1967 thru 1972, a great divide of the mind, had established itself in America, and I was planted in the future. A time traveler in generational ethos. Younger, much younger, though I did not know it, and received by the inhabitants of the Ballfields and the Grassy Knoll of Jackson Pond. For these people, I am grateful. They gave me what few ever have: a Home away from home. A base for my feet to stand, and for me to slowly recover some balance.

This ability was intrinsic to these dwellers, though I give a lot of credit to the place itself, with it's towering backdrop of pines and sheltering barrier fences and Concrete walls. The design of Jackson Pond Park was done by Olmstead, the same one who brought Central Park its Wonders. Perhaps many years later, he assisted the return of one Veteran. Thanks from me to all, for launching the reborn child into his new life at Home.

Chapter E: Billy Plays the Hill

1976, maybe August. Jackson Pond Story,   Billy C. plays the hill.

This will be so simple to see, for those who know Jackson Pond. I have been going to this part of the Park since I Chased Rosalie and had my Hockey Skates.

Once, an actual man-made, concrete, water feature of Forest Park, "The Pond" had become a dry asphalt and concrete oval, with a low wall all around the perimeter. The central area was a great, undefined place to play all kinds of games. Large enough for excellent touch football, wide enough for a full basketball court, and long enough for stickball the long way. ALMOST.

The beauty of the area is the rising bowl shape that the surrounding hills provide. The North side has a second retaining wall, under a magnificent pine grove. This borders your left side, as you face East.   Home plate is down in the corner, on the West side of the Pond. You hit toward the East, a right hand batter will have the pines at his back. You have an open space in front, and to your southerly view is, right field. The right field "line", is imaginary, as is most of the field.   The ball is thrown up by the batter, or bounced by a pitcher. The idea of the field, and the game is to hit to straight away center only.   Automatics, is the name of the game, no base running. If your shot lands inside the Imaginary field, you get the base according to distance.

The defensive players must catch everything on a fly. Pretty simple, for the first 200 feet of "pond".   At that point the northern wall begins to curve into the field, from left to right when seen from Home Plate, and continues, as a pond will, to wrap clean through the field, forming a boundry about two feet high.   Hard to picture how guys can play fly balls, with this at the back of their field , yes?

Well, that is only the first base, as it were, of the "Pond Stickball field".   Above this lower deck, curving around from the left, is the sidewalk of the original pond design. The place where people enjoyed the pastoral setting and weeping willows, as the children floated boats. The trees that once stood here are long gone. There are some benches to complicate things, maybe some people too.

The ball lands there- That's a Double.

Above this, is our curving knoll of grass, the Triple area.   Ranging in height from four feet to sixteen feet, this sloping area of field is referred to as "the hill".

Without further area, no field would be complete, but never fear.   Above this curving knoll, we have: The street.   There may or may not be traffic;, there is definitely a hill sloping down from your right, as you face home plate, and one sloping down in front as well. There is a sidewalk, and curbing, too.   Overhead, hang two large trees. If the ball lands here, it is a Home Run! Pretty simple really.   You are standing, in the Street, 200 feet from Home, under trees, with a steep grassy hill, right in front of you, trying to catch fly balls.

    AND, if you are trying to chase the ball through these last two places, you are, "Playing the Hill."

    Straight to the point, now that you know where we are. Playing stick at the Pond, is a regular way to compete, drink, and pass the summer afternoons. The intensity ranges from guys who never go out in the field...just get their "ups", to players who will run head first into the myriad, awkward places, trying to make a catch. Neither of these is usually remarkable; the way of the Pond is the way of the careless warrior. You were just, AT, the Pond.

    One thing that is universal to sport is positional ranking.   The best players do not play in right field, or bat last. The Long Way stickball equivalent of top dog position is "Playing the Hill."   Everyone gets a try at it, sure.   Sometimes, there are three or four guys on the hill.   This is not when the games are serious.   Then, the plays you make are too difficult and hilariously heroic, to be left to chance.   After all, they're Homers and Triples.   Though I've tried to do it, the position is much better left to the three or four top stickballers at the Pond, and one of these is, Billy C.

    There are two very distinct sets of guys at the Pond, us, and the young guys. Us, are a group of eighteen year olds, and me, Old Mike.   Maybe they are twenty.   We got, Pete and Phil, and Tilly and Brian, as lead dogs. They can play any sport, and have plenty of Richmond Hill credentials. The young guys are maybe, the little brothers, or underclassmates of the Us.   Forgive me, not knowing the ages so well, I am 24 years old, having wasted a couple of years getting drafted. So much older than anybody in a park should ever be.

The young guys got Glenn and Tommy, and Billy C.   This is Billy C's story.

There are some big guys in the park, none seems bigger than Billy, though some actually are.

People have lots of fun here, Billy is in the middle of all of it, or he is the first one they want to tell about whatever did happen. He is a player so crafty at our games, that he can always find a way around, or over, or behind you. Not that he couldn't go right through! He is here for his friends, always , and everyone here is his friend. I might say, Billy is the complete, American Billy, with a small side of tony.

Billy Plays the Hill.

Today, me and our boy, are on the same team, for long way stickball. Billy is behind me, up top. I am playing on the sidewalk, below, at the bottom of the knolly hill of grass. The game is, steady serious. Brian is up at bat, a big hitter, who moves you back in anticipation of the Homer. One out, there are never any baserunners. Brian tosses the ball out in front of him, and lets it take one bounce, as he rears the bat back, to take a slash at the descending arc of the dropping toss...his cut catching the ball, dead square, middle of the round bat, flat and lining, a curling, knuckling drive over the infielders, and rising. This should be my play, down low, except the ball continues to rise, toward the base of the knoll. Over my head it cranks, and dives, from the terrific spin. It looks like a Triple for sure; except here comes Billy, sliding down the hill. One leg out in front, one curled under. He is, baseball style sliding, to make a play at the bottom of the grass. And! He makes it, what a catch! Brian must be shocked, his Triple is an Out. But, Billy looks a little worried?

"Mike, I think I cut my leg," says Billy, with a puzzled look on his face, not pain, more like curiousity.

I can see his pants are sliced cleanly, up the side of his calf and knee. Opening the cloth, I see the same effect underneath. Billy has a surgical looking slice of about three inches long, that has completely opened his knee joint, until you can see the white gristle. There is virtually no bleeding. This odd injury is bizarre to look at, for sure. Billy has been relying on my observation until he makes the mistake of...taking a peek! His eyes looked down; then at me, for a brief moment, and then, they rolled right up and out of sight! He didn't pass out, but close. Cannot blame him, it looked awful.

There was no way for me to clean, or dress the wound, so I pressed down on the two sides and, pushed them back together. While pressing, I folded the pants back over likewise, and pressed those. Suddenly, remembering what a selfish guy I am, I got Steven to hold and press in my place.

Off to the Doctors, in a friend's car, went Billy with Steven attached. They were already laughing it off, I think Billy wanted to keep playing! The whole thing is just the way Billy always was, ready and able. Alive and well.

I was so interested to hear how the injury came out, and when I did hear, it was so good. The close up job, worked great. A stitch or two, and back to the park. Billy was one of the people who helped me feel this was home, at a time when that helped close up my wounds, just as neat.

Chapter F: First Job On Fire

Employed, 1972

In 1972, through an acquaintance of my Uncle Bill, a carpenter for the N.Y.C. Board of Education, I obtained the job of cleaner, in a Public School, in East New York, Brooklyn. Very ready to be employed, due to being so broke, I didn't let the terrible neighborhood deter me.

Before starting, my new boss Mr. Ellis had me visit his office. His main helper, Billy, told me to "bring a gun" cause the job would be gang turf. The Sheffield Projects, where the school was located was "tomahawk turf". This was cruel to say, to a new guy, yes. . . but the general feeling among custodial staffs said, "East NY is a war zone." The vandalism and break-ins made the 75th precinct, a busy place.

You could imagine the work to be simple, yes and not very interesting , but one craft being practiced in about half of NYC public schools, was fascinating to me. Firing Coal Boilers.

Actually, physical labor or work of any kind was new to me, and I would learn many skills during my time caring for school buildings. There are many "tricks of the trade" in maintaining large and aging schools, but none had the spirit and soul of tending fire. The first time, my fireman, Louie pushed those glowing coals with the heavy, long metal hoe, to prepare and manage the coal fire under that boiler, I realized something beautiful was being done.

That fire, had been ignited in early September. My first day of work was Dec. 20th. Louie and his son, Maxwell, had cared for that spark every day and hour since. Using it daily to provide heat. Feeding the coal through the twin, cast iron doors, spreading the fuel with the flip of a shovel to keep the uniform burn across the surface, controlling the flow of air from under and above. Cleaning the ashes produced by pushing the burning char back and forth, and dumping the ash to the pit below by the movable grates.

Exhorting and accelerating the combustion, until the boilers drank enough of that plasma to produce steam. Satisfying the heating needs, then slowing the pace of combustion with the draft dampers, as necessary. At the end of the day. . . banking the fire, as if, to a magic sleep state, by shaping and covering, and slowing the passage of air. The fire will slow until almost inactive, and remain in that state overnight. Pulsing slowly, under the blanket of coal, hungry for the Oxygen to free it. Caution!! - this process produces mucho carbon monoxide. For that fire is in no way OUT, only at bay, controlled. Ready to spring up at the introduction of draft, air-fresh and clean in the morning . There was a soul to it, that I found magical.

I had my chance at this trade quite soon and spent seven years at it.

Learning the craft at this 80,000 sq. ft. school put me into the Job at Jefferson High School, a huge 450,000 sq. ft. Relic that burned coal in Huge Locomotive Type Boilers. We went through 900 tons a year, 1,800,000 lbs taken by shovel, into the Coal Bucket and Hoisted, dropped in piles in front of the Fireboxes, shoveled across the surface of glowing embers, pushed about to suit the needs of the heat load, dropped as ash to the pits below and shoveled into big ribbed cans for disposal. Fireman was the Title, it paid a little extra. We each cleaned three fireboxes a day, me and Johnny Manzella.

Frantically pushing with the Hoe, a steel rod of twelve feet with a flat slab at the business end, to maintain the fire and keep pressure on the system. Dropping the slag to the pit with levers controlling the grates of the Firebed. I liked it, actually. The intensity was nice to experience. I felt all studly. I was craving, just hungry to flex myself, if that explains it. The hardness of me needed burning. Tempering. My lungs suffered, my soul breathed.

Chapter G: Dream Talk

Dreamy Compliment. Morning Chatter in the Office of my School. 1990

My job has the interesting aspect of giving service to a mainly female population.

You are one of very few males to pass through the day to day existence of Teachers. Often times, these daily interactions become a part of the deep psyche.

Dreams, often contain places and people familiar to the dreamer, in oddly changed ways, and this is what Mrs. Baez told us, this morning.

 "Oh, Mr. Schneider, you appeared in my dream last night"; this causing the assembled group of office staff and teachers to giggle.   "Of course, we see each other every day, and I do appear in many dreams, " I say, being both gentlemanly and cute. This is actually true, as reported by many teachers over the years.   I continued by saying, "I dream consistently of the buildings I've maintained, and the people in them."

 "That may be true, Mike," said Mrs. B, "but in my dream, you spoke perfect Spanish."

 I was so flattered, I blushed.

Chapter H: Temporary Care

1997, On the job, NYC School Custodian

Temporary Care Assignment, at P.S .99 Queens

More than 1,300 children and 200 staff at this large grammar school, up to the sixth grade in a nice neighborhood , called Kew Gardens, is a place for me to make extra money for a few weeks.   A Perk of my job that allows/avoids the hiring of Temporary employees to cover open positions.   Twenty four hour care without hiring any replacement for the Board of Ed, and an extra salary for me.   The regular school I supervise would be fine with a little less attention for eight weeks. This new place is full of teachers and children with interesting stories, none of my business. My part here is to insure the operation continues to cause no problems to those real people.

Custodial staffs, in short are best when seen least . Schools do take lots of attention, they are full of needy people.   The men who work in them often gain too much discretion because of this imbalanced relationship, and act out in unpleasant ways. This is unacceptable and I do not permit it.   The actual supervisors in my job are allowing much too much of this power playing crap.   It is common for two reasons. One reason is the weakness of some bosses; they cannot control themselves and sell out to the help to cover up.   You can hardly preach to guys who know your corruption.

Second, and much worse, are those bosses using the helpers to intimidate the poor defenseless women working in their schools.   I make it sound as evil as possible because it IS a rancid reversal of manliness.   Custodians and their staff members are Union protected. If they simply care for the chores and do the maintenance and paperwork, they may work peacefully in a school for many years.   Instead, quite a few use this security blanket to smother legitimate complaints, expending energy avoiding the proper procedures necessary to maintain a large building.

My temporary assignment has sunken to this level. The helpers disrespect everyone from the Principal on down. The previous boss engaged in personal negligence and laziness, turning the keys over, as it were, to his lead dog, the school fireman/ boiler tender.   Mistake number one, compounded by his man being a classic stereotype of a resenter.   These guys are deeply angry and insecure.   The American prejudice against janitors is eagle-like in acceptance.   This is a truly mindless tenet of society. Americans think cleaning and maintenance work is beneath them. Just the opposite will always be true. Holding the fort against the forces of entropy is obviously noble work. In the face of the wasteful, carefree American's usage or abusage of public buildings, it's quite a source of pride to even maintain conditions. At times, my buildings have actually improved or been restored by my staff. These thoughts are way beyond my new Fireman at P.S. 99.

No, this fellow needs flattening. He will resist and have some success. He will know limits are in place. We will work on temporary surfaces created by me. I begin flattening this guy immediately. Best way to do this is touring the facility with him. If his interest is where it should be and his physical plant is well maintained, he can pretty much tell me to drop dead. Happy to drop dead for such performance am I. Nothing else is required, disrespecting me being out of the question.

Knowing what will be the results of this tour, he tries to be busy with other matters. There are no other matters! He will tour with me. Dragging him from machine room, to boiler room, to roof and yard reveals absolute negligence and incompetence. Worse than I suspected, I had to close the schoolyard due to collapsing coping stones and decorative caps, and the corners hanging loosely above. Some are held in place by ropes! I am pretty furious; can't even finish my inspection before having to go to the Principal and call the Central office supervision for help.

Neither is happy with me. I do not care. I inform the Principal, "the yard is closed". He sputters his protest. I do not care. Downtown supervision wants to counsel me on protocol and procedure, I do not care. They are coming out tomorrow morning, with the stonemasons, because I have closed the yard. They have no choice because I do not give away the keys. We are not supposed to let people get killed - that's a rule I made up.

There are some other troubles here that I can act on, with my staff. Others, I gotta eat them because of the fuss over the parapet walls and my swift actions against the staff attitude problem. The parapet problems were so bad that I really sold out with the supervisors. Really banging hard on the safety drum. They aren't gonna' give me anything else. I know well, this school is beyond my short term whipping. You also have to watch out the crew doesn't go mad, or sometimes that can get you buried. The Custodial workers are very tense already, having the awful surge of fear that accompanies exposing it to Higher levels of scrutiny. Giving you this background, lets you picture my reaction to this next and most curious problem. One I had never seen before.

This school was heated by two large oil burners. They were not new but they were plenty powerful enough for the work. These burners used Number 6 oil. A type of oil thicker than the home heating oil that burns automatically and somewhat unnoticed in the average home. This stuff, is closer to crude oil. It is what is left once the lighter fuels are extracted from what comes out of the ground. It must be filtered, as it contains tars. The stuff will remain almost solid until it is heated enough to flow, then be pumped at pressure, and burned. Low in BTU content and high in sulfates, the emissions are sometimes bad, sometimes downright awful. This describes the routine results of #6 oil combustion.

Now, this helper I have described as such scum makes these boilers work under some relatively unpleasant conditions. He knows the tricks of the trade, as he has learned them right here for the last nineteen years. It is an important and impressive task, the sort of special skill used to intimidate the uninformed. He is better than me at this, way better. About 98 % of those benefitted by modern HVAC systems have little idea what the hell is actually going on downstairs, so to speak. This is the reason Plumbers can tell you anything, as you nod approval. Same as car mechanics who bamboozle everyone who never gets their hands dirty, these guys are engaged in class warfare. They don't need to win the war, as long as they win every battle. But my man here is losing this battle with these boilers, because of the tremendous amount of trouble with the last load of #6 oil delivered. Three thousand gallons, which entered his fuel tank about ten days prior. He has already burned about half and it has been a bitch of a time. The filters are clogged over and over with heavy tars and material which isn't even familiar to him. The combustion alarms go off from the smoke conditions. The stuff smells acrid and makes him nauseous.

In the face of this, my operator is performing so well that nobody else is aware. The last boss was leaving and ignored the boiler room, just like the roof. Makes me more angry than anything helpers do. Too many who have risen to the supervision from the scut level turn a blind eye where they could do so much good, without any trouble. The resentments and indignities of the service industry produce a bitter attitude among workers, who experience an arrogant and dismissive public. This story recalls many dogs who had their day. Our dogs here, myself included, will not!

My expertise is not up to par on this dirty oil topic, and I sincerely want to help and follow up the best I can. I have been a beast about everything else, toward the my help, AND the upper bosses. There is much more to my mans' story. The Oil was pumped in and no bill was left in an unusual, overnight delivery. An odd thing in itself, as the stuff cost a dollar a gallon. Seems the apartment building next door also uses #6 oil, my operator has received mistakenly delivered oil in the past. A huge apartment complex could receive such a large amount of fuel explaining the anonymous load, but that doesn't explain two things: Why is this fuel so damn toxic, and WHY have they not come looking for it. Nobody waits a month to get paid for oil in the middle of winter. I am convinced something serious is wrong; and I have a scary suspicion.

The NYC Board of Ed. has a Fuel Division, the people who we call for deliveries, and issues such as this. I have not dealt with them on this problem or anything else too large in my 25 years with the Board. Most of my time has been in schools using coal for heating, not uncommon at all in the seventies and eighties, and a story itself. Fuel Division is independent from my side of the business, and I have no pull or standing with them. They could tell me to drop dead, especially because oil is not my thing. It would be easy to embarass myself, talking to people who arrange a million gallons a month. That exact type of thought has gotten many Custodians burned. Not me!! my mentors in this business always said, "The only stupid questions are the ones you don't ask!"

On the phone with Fuel, these guys are probably the largest fuel buyers in the City of N.Y. my attention is sharp. My suspicions are also tempering my questions, as I describe my understanding of how bad this #6 oil is, to the guy from downtown. To my thinking, everyone downtown is my boss. Once again, I am taking the stance that "action must be taken." I am requesting they pump the tank out, period. The response is that the oil is not his, why should he do anything ? If I would have said up front, NO HEAT, he would have been stuck. Rookie mistake by me and strike one. He knew it was half gone 'cause I told him. He knew there was no bill 'cause I told him . Strike two. Not knowing where else to voice my opinion, my suspicions were next on this clipboard of misplaced modifiers.

"I think," says I, to the downtown guy, "This oil has not been misplaced. It has been made to burn like sticky paste, has been dumped in our tank with great haste, It is not fuel, but Oily Waste." In short a toxic waste collector has purposely injected this stuff and your poor employee has been suffering the consequences along with the surrounding neighbors. Strike three !!

My supposed boss on the phone suggests I follow up on this idea! As if this is a scenario unheard of by anyone on the reality side . This is like Strike Four!!!!

I realize that I am standing on the tracks, here comes the Bright Light. On the other end of this phone is the engineer. Yes, I should pursue this further!!!

As a lifelong New Yorker, one must be able to realize when the train is coming and stand aside. Ole'.

Chapter I: Big Mike

May, 1992, at Kissena Lake

"Big Mike"

We go fishin', my two kids and me. We hop in the car, with the poles and go. When I was a child, this would have been very different, like an event. As an adult, I take these two all the time. Supply the action, Dad.

Amy has been at this since she was five, half her life. Mike started just as young, he's seven. We catch tiny fish, with bread as bait, and throw them back. The kids have contests, trying to catch the most. If it rains at the lake, we play baseball in the car, until it lets up. Three happy children, leaving Mom at home. We have fished way past the limit, for Mom. Surprisingly, I know very little about fishing. The outdoorsman in NYC is hard pressed to become experienced on the "Daniel Boone" level. Studying the subject seems a wacky activity, just let the fish do the talking.

We are enthusiastic about it...the surroundings, the company, the whole bucket is great fun. There are turtles and frogs, and terrific birds to enjoy.

I pop lures through the fresh water, while they catch sunnys and bluegills. I use the same ones here, as I use in the salt water, for larger species. Lighter rod, reel and line here for much smaller fish. I am not the pro shop angler and that suits me fine.

This perfect, bright, warm day, I am flipping a , "Bomber, Long A" lure. Comically, it is about as long as the fish the contest is yielding. We can see some Carp, flapping about; they are big, very big, but not "game fish". They feed slowly and lazily. Game fish are ready to strike their prey, making for an actual sporting interest in the species. Predators vying for survival.

Water roiling, about twenty feet out, provokes my casting the 'bomber ' onto the spot. Snagging fish, by jerking the hooks into them, is very poor form for catch and release anglers. I am not trying to do anything like that to the Carp, only catch the small bass that are captive here. Most are about two pounds, or much less. I have never seen any larger ones, here or anywhere else.

After one quick tug on the pole, the tip bends sharp and hard. Hesitating to yank and snag myself further, I give it a slight pull, side ways. Clunk, that rod is heavy and full of life. This feeling is surprising, almost impossible to believe. The weight and fight in my hands is making me nervous. My kids know, right away , something is up. The motion and action in the water has alerted them. This is a big, big, fish, probably, definitely, big. Then, as I hold a firm steady grip to test the fight,   the line looses pressure. I back up a bit and stop, feeling what seems to be a snag on a heavy, inert object. Moments ago there was a fish, now there is the dead weight of a tree limb, or the classic tire.

 The kids are watching and a few others, as well. Have I really made this mistake? NO, that is a crafty old fish trick, I am feeling, on the far end of this line. Dive under that structure and sit. Am I a fish mind-reader, mind-reading my fish, or silly ?

 I have decided to wait this out. The lure may be stuck fast; I cannot move it with the regular line snapping tricks,   so I wait. Both kids go back to dipping bread, while keeping an eye on me.   Amy is not serious about fishing;   we have been joking about the original tiny fish, we first caught, for years. Nappers and Loopers we called them. Smaller versions of the Bluefish and Flounder of Jamaica Bay, where we first wet the lines. She has fun doing anything with me.   Mike is a seven year old future pro, serious about most of his hobbies. On this matter, they agree; Dad is acting foolish.   The spectators wander off, as well. Minutes pass as the line pressure stays just the same. Just the same, just the sloosh and swing left. That clever trickster ran out of patience, and left the snag to flee. Nope, the hook is set, and the distance is shrinking. Soon, next to the concrete pond rim, his full measure is revealed.   My kids grab the rod, while I lift this whopper bass out into the air.   We, three, are behaving like people who caught a big fish.   Impressive, considering we are shocked at this thing coming into our tiny fishtown !!

 "Big Mike" is this; a Tail, that is about the size of a hand, a Body, that looks like a volley ball, and a Gaping Mouth, the size of your face.   You can see down that maw six inches. He is about twenty inches long, maybe longer, and weighs about eight pounds. It...is...a largemouth bass, unlike anything I have seen before. We three are so thrilled, yet anxious to release our legend to his world.   Soon enough, he splashed away and we were alone again. In a way.

 This stayed with us in a family way. We named our "Big Mike" that day, and referred to him many times. Not long after this magic day, Amy stopped going fishing with Daddy. Mike, my son, not the fish, knocked around the shoreline with me many more times before being too grown up for it. Be There, my friend, Big Mike, Forever in our Minds.

 P.S. the largest fish are usually the females.

Chapter J: Float in a Boat

The Island, 1992, The Float, in the Boat.

They have a saying , "You are Rhode Island Born and Rhode Island bred. And then when you die, You are Rhode Island Dead." We just Visited.

We go to Rhode Island, every summer, now, with our children. Our dear friend, Kathy invites us, to stay on "The Island". The perfection of the setting is only the same as the lovely people who are with me. My wife and perfect partner, my daughter, and my eight year old son.

The wife, is so far superior to myself, in every way. Her appearance is the exact vision of her times. Her attitude and intellect are fiercely independent. I love her, the entire day and night.

I am always happy to try pleasing her. This is sometimes, quite easy. She plans and prepares every aspect of our trips, and makes notes, as we travel. Myself, I get in the car and drive. The kids are travel friendly. There are so many nice pastimes for all of us, in the town of Westerly. The local store has Blueberry pie, the local paper has interesting Real Estate, the arcade has Pool Tables and games; there is shopping, and restaurants, so much.

But for me, and my two buddies, one thing makes the Island extra special terrific,

A Float in The Boat. The kids are 11 and 8, they've been coming here for four years, and love the fourteen foot, fiberglas composite Rowboat, that we take out into the salty, shallow, and calm Bay waters that surround our summer place. The Island itself, is on Shore Road, a well known byway, Scenic 1A, next to a string of lovely homes, golf courses, and tiny baylets. These Baylets, all reaching in, toward the Western mainland. They open on their East sides to a much larger channel, running North/South, that Channel bordered by a barrier Island. The barrier Island holds the Misquamicut beaches, which face the Atlantic Ocean. The great Hurricane of 1939 had washed, or more like flew, houses clean across that Channel, and on to the Mainland. Most summer days, all the sheltered waters behind the barrier, were calm, ideal to Float in any Boat.

The Island had a tiny driveway, constructed by the owners, OG Rhode Islanders, years earlier. You approached this hatchway, which was usually almost covered by bushes and vines, from the West, making a sharp right turn. Descending a rapid chute of grassy hill. Now, at the base, you could cross the single car width bridge. This transition, in a matter of 100 feet, deposited your mind in another realm. One of Herons and Phragmites, ripples and briny air. Where the woodchucks sniffed and ducked, and the ducks turned their heads, reluctantly toward your intrusive self. The domain of the Swans and tiny songbirds. The summer home of dreams, the base camp of the Floats.

My wonderful wife could not enjoy the Floats, they gave her the willys. So, it would always be Dad, Amy, and Michael, off to spend a magic time, slowly and silently, skimming the outer reaches of our shoreline. Searching for the wildlife, that lived all around this mini- paradise. The circle of shore defining the waterline, was no more than 300 feet, from North, rotating South. Our vessel, always awaited its crew, on the starboard side, or maybe the port side, I don't know. On the left, anyway, the Captain just needs to get the life jackets on, and push, and row. Push off, depart the land, and feel the float. The levitating, bouncing under your feet, shifting. The Floating of the Boat, with the Buddies.

Amy was the picture of happiness and childlike beauty, able to handle every toss and turn of the boat, or life. Smart, like her Mom and kind, loving, cheerfully happy, calm, and funny. Super long hair and a smile, of glowing love, she could have never been any more perfect, to her Dad. She enjoyed the sights and sounds, with curiousity, and a knowledge of what a special place the Island actually was. The people in the area called this property, "The house on the Island", not because of the house, which was modest, but because of the perfectly wrought location. The most scenic and quaint view, on a scenic, A' road. Amy belonged as " the kid" who people imagined lived there, as they drove by, seeing the sights, and dreaming of such a vacation.

Mike was our hunter, a city boy, born with a country instinct. His love for the things he was pursuing, made you proud. His bush of red hair, leaning over the prow of our slowly moving, blue and white craft, loomed above a sea of tiny creatures, and Large dreams. We did catch some hefty, Striped Bass, fishing from our Rowboat. A couple took us for the mini version of the "Nantucket Sleighride", but the most fun of all the denizens we chased were the crabs. Fun to stalk, as you silently hovered and maneuvered, and big silly fun to catch, or try to catch. Lots of them got away, We let all of them go, anyway. The greatest kicks, for all of us, would be Mike reaching down, and picking them with bare hands, almost always resulting in some wobbling and yelling, if not the classic, finger pinch. How studiously, we peered into those, two or three feet of water. Hugging the shore and inching forward. Amy was able to see them fine, but Mike always picked them.   She used the net, which was made for swimming crabs and fish.   Mike always picked them.

Each year, we went, each year, our friend invited us, each of us, learning to love, learning what family can mean, and how great a friend can be.   For me, it was one great meeting after another. One wonderful and loving person entering my life, after another. Blessings accumulating, for myself and my loving wife.   We lost that dear friend, who had given my little group, those immensely precious days. How much she meant to us. No more, do we " Float in the Boat"   No more.

But,   I hope some day, and I hope it sincerely, that,   we will do, just that, with our friends and our family, again.

Chapter K: Medallion

Medallion

People are so stylish in NYC. If you pay attention.

It's been a while since I regularly rode the NYC subways. Never was my favorite thing. Once upon a trip home from work, on the E train, which travels under Queens Boulevard, I noticed a very tired lady, across from me. Her age and appearance were mostly, unremarkable. She seemed an average commuter. An interesting design on the left lapel of her coat, caught my eye, sort of a Cameo shaped Medallion, of about four inches in length. It shimmered in the light, although darker than the rest of her coat. What really caught my eye was the shiny, nearly moving center. Seeming to shimmer, in the light, although darker than the rest of the coat.

As I puzzled about it, the woman was falling asleep. As she did, her head nodded, toward her left and, down came the drool. Right smack into the fancy design, I'd noticed. Yes, it shimmered, and ran, and helped reveal the clever style, of this tired commuter!

Chapter L: Coney Island Summer

Coney Island Summer, Handball Mecca, 2014   ,

These are my boys on my courts, playing, like children, carrying lives many decades long.

Thinking only, of this world, held loosely, between these yellow lines and concretely,

before this 14 foot wall, this repainted, sunburned tower face. TRYING,

to simply, Chase, only the points to score, only the ball to retrieve, simply the next sharp

serve to snap off, essentially moments of, immortality

Draw the sandy air, into lungs: partial breathe into, Hi-mile lungs.

Sweat, hard thru skin of leathery age. Run hard, and swing sharp, Just to,

Defy the conditions of time and space, upon their actions and mortality.

RISE, above- exceed and deny it ! Hold it all at bay, far outside the game.

Admire these candles, burning in the ocean breeze.

May they live forever, and have a good partner, to blame it on.

Chapter M: Where Went My Friend?

Where went my friend ? The story of release and commitment.

There were two fellas, who met a time ago, their lives I'd say, were less than presidential. Upon a time of penancem they gained acquaintance, they were corrections residential.

And among the many, who crossed the paths of our rogues, many were those, they'd robbed. Away so far, from the child within, few were those who sobbed. And hardened as such, by the price for their vice, they peered through slitted eye, at another kindred soul of clouds, who might just be, a friend of I . Might trust and share, and give thanks for themselves, who had been given years to be on shelves, who now removed, from sky and life, who now cannot see, their Dads' wife, whose famililies, show up no more, might simply find a friend once more, might chance to be a friend, once more.

Now these two likely fellows shared the cell, the meals, the time now spared. To be one friend, to another such, if not their worlds of hope, to touch. The gift undeserved, they valued high, as seventeen years went by.

And on that day, when one came free, they both felt captive, and free. These men now of age, had no choice, and turned another page. Our free man surged to life anew, and became a friend to many who, remarked his honor and held him high, as he always remembered the reason why. He had learned of things that set him well, from the days with other, of the cell.   And he kept up touch, with visit or call, with the other side of the prison wall. Over time the calls were fewer, still the closeness was , and always will. Came a day on computer, our free man, a status he sought, found released as the word the system brought, and an anger came in a flash, he thought, " has this been what years of friendship bought," that his partner of time should be beyond those walls, and free. And not to reach right out to me!

Released it said, and this was true. He later discovered on further review. His term of life was satisfied,   his friend for life had justly died, and on prison rolls he was not deceased, he had Finally;   been released.

Chapter N: Apple a Day

June of 1986,   An Apple a Day

Once upon a time in the land of Ridgewood , Queens, I took care of a Public School and the People in it.   The Building sat up on a rise, on Fresh Pond Road. Perhaps, 80 years earlier, there was a pond, next to a lovely, tall, red brick building. No more, now the fading face of the Southern side of my school, surveyed a dry land. The Rooftop View was Tremendous, all the way to Jamaica Bay. To the West, Manhattan and beyond, RIDGE wood, by name and standing.

New York City Schools had become extremely crowded and nearly antiquated. This one had a thousand children, packed into about thirty-five usable rooms. The roof leaked and plaster was leaving the walls in chips and chunks. My crew regularly prodded and poked the window poles into the upper corners on the fourth floor, knocking huge plaster chunks off, before they just plain fell.

The heat was supplied by coal from a Boiler room rife with friable asbestos. There was no gym and the lunchroom did triple duty as a multi-purpose space. No elevator, of course. All this, was pretty typical, as was the staff of well educated teachers. From my unique vantage point, it was easy to see that teaching is a very lonely affair. Once that classroom door slams shut, you're flying solo in uncertain weather. People may have misunderstood me, when I said, that these teachers got more support from me saying hello, than any other source. Often times, when something called for me to be present in a class, I became invisible, as I monitored a heat loss, or worked on a leak. The students and teacher would proceed, allowing me to observe the reality of the teaching job. My belief that teaching is a gift, never wavered, and as time passed, I learned one thing. That space and those children become the whole of reality, for a real teacher. When they report that a shade, or a noise, or the door is driving them insane, it is the Only Shade, the Only Door, in their universe. Take it serious, Mr. Service Guy. Anyhow....

Fresh Pond Road was a terrific shopping area, I could get great deli food, or Clothing from China. Fruits and vegetables...the hardware store sold train sets. Man, the place had it all, on the Mom and Pop level. Teachers would often hustle out to shop during breaks; they always seemed so harried. The teachers lunchroom was a sad set of orange topped tables and student chairs, but most faculty gathered with their fellows during the two periods when all the students ate.   Perfect to allow my plan "To Apple the Staff".

 Having all the keys, and the forty apples by 11:00 A.M., I popped into each classroom and placed an apple on the teachers' desks, in their absence. Taking about fifteen minutes and costing about three bucks, this gave me so much enjoyment.   Feeling really good about the secretive act of support and the classic " apple for the teacher" aspect, I retired to my office to await...the feedback.   You can imagine the various reactions from the different people, "How Nice!" or "This is Odd." or " What the Heck?", I expected to hear some funny things, as well as getting to show how a tiny gesture, might be so significant. Well...

 After a short time, I began to realize that not one teacher had even noticed the apples' appearances.   No amount of inquiry produced a murmur.   This group was just that "locked in" on their performance.   The Invisible Apples.

Chapter O: King Democrat

Vote Aqui, Here, and not Here.

Tomorrow, Tuesday, I will go to my polling place, up the block, and Vote. This time my exciting choices will be in the Democratic Primary. I have always been one of the Donkey Clan. The home I now live in, is one block away from my childhood home. I can see the attic window that I boarded up over there, from my stoop. Because of this penchant for world travel, I have always voted at the Public School, up the block. We always say "Up the Block". New Yorkers always say Up, Down, Across, etc. when referring to places. No one else knows which way that means, but if you say Up Town, everyone knows you do not mean anywhere in Queens or Brooklyn. We go "Over" to the City, when we go to Manhattan, or "Out" on the Island, meaning East. P.S. 90 is "UP" like Canada.

Besides playing in the yard there as a little guy, I was the Custodian there for 18 years. The job was great, right up the block from my house when my kids were little. So, I Voted in the same place where it was my job to help run the Polling Site. In addition to this, the Election was considered an "Outside Activity" by NYC Board of ED and the Poll Site Supervisor had to sign my Space Sheets for the Day. I guess you can see how deeply wrapped up in the thing I was. The day the Towers got hit, I was having a local election in my School, they shut that down in concern for safety, but I thought it the wrong choice.

My job, here in my Hometown, meant a lot to me. My crew was able to make lots of improvements to the Old Barn. Nothing stood in the way, if you cared about Buildings and people. Fighting to restore or renew the physical plant gave me pride and bolstered my workers self esteem. They would sometimes hustle to finish the routine chores, in order to "get after" whatever project we had going. We reinstalled the Old Brass that had been put aside, and refinished surfaces that had been converted for convenience. We did specialty painting, though that is a tricky business. One summer we did the Entire 80 feet of the First Floor Corridor Walls in High White Gloss and People said it looked like a Hospital. Anyway. . .

After about 12 years of working and voting and after, 50 years of being districted to do that, the thing that we call Government decided that redistricting was in order and informed me that I now belonged "Down" at P.S. 62. Besides the aggravating thoughts of the "why" of it, my cranky mind held an inate prejudice and a selfish notion of propriety. Bluntly put, I was outraged! This was the Pearl Harbor of Civic Insults. Sending the Exalted ME, from my Kingdom of Democracy to go Down, down, down.

Unfair, I commited no crime, why was I banished?   Who allowed this to happen? To say that I was a bit spoiled was insufficient. I did recover enough to continue casting my Votes in the new place.   Walking in there did make me feel small and insignificant, which is no fun. Sometimes you wanna' go, where everybody knows your name.

  Within a few years, this was rectified and my just place as Election Boy was restored. VOTE.

Chapter P: Mike Smiles

January, 2015

   Syosset, New York, Entered in a Four Wall Handball Tournament.
I am participating in another singles event, in my age group, at this beautiful health club and gym, on Long Island. Sixty Five years old, I play in a division called: Super Golden Masters.   Lots of guys are actually, just that. They have been involved in Handball their whole lives, at a championship level. Not me, I only started, fifteen years ago when I quit basketball and my son took up this sport.

   As a young and fit starter, Mike Jr. made progress rapidly, to the highest level. Succeeding in many ways, and winning pretty regularly.

   As an older and less physical competitor, my progress was slow, but sure. Each year, brought me closer to the plateau, where the veteran players reside. Earning the chance "to belong," in games where you must produce results, or be eliminated and shunned. Older players demand competence from the accepted crew. There are some social aspects to this clique type behavior. Those are not what matters most. The freight, in these games, is the ability to raise your game, to test the best. This past couple of years, I am in those "best games." Testing myself against champs with dozens of National Championships in the one wall sport. For me, this is like " teeing it up with Tiger" for free. The games at Coney Island have improved my overall game plenty.

   In summation of my Titles; I have never won a singles event of any kind, excepting once. That was a park tournament where my opponent stole the trophy - I was 16!

   So, the Long Island Open was the sort of opportunity that I've rarely had before, and might never get again. They have age groups older than 60's. Even at 60, you must realize what a winner you are, simply to be participating. At 70+ , well, fitness is just a gift. There are serious competitions at that level, between determined and strong guys, These are often shocking to the casual observer. Age groupers are very dedicated, or they would disappear. Your fellow players will happily slaughter you, should you show up inept, or out of shape. Handball, a place where good sportsmanship is common, is essentially a brutish combat sport. It took quite a while for me to adjust. The attitude of super competitive athletes, is robotic in nature; repetitive, driven, even greedy. Seeking advantage at all times, without respite. It's nuts!

I never will have the complete mental strength of some fellows that I've known. That may be a gift, or a curse. Do I desire to make sporting goals a destination and my mentality just, a vehicle ? In some ways, I have always done this, to a point, without accepting the chalice of fervent commitment. In an aside, I wonder if it is possible that such drive, is actually inate. Considering the countless serious games, leagues, and efforts I've totaled; I am committed to the sporting challenge, lifestyle wise. My best efforts have rarely included the driven attitude encountered, in the few I've mentioned here.

Fortunate, as always, I felt fit for the weekend of Syosset. Never had any injury crop up during a scheduled tourney, I try to train and play my way into shape for each big event. Especially, the One Wall Nationals at Coney Island, as well as the big indoor tourneys, of the Four Wall season. Some confusion arose, about my entrance into the proper age group. This delayed the set up of my first round time and opponent. I am scheduled to play a local, Long Island fellow, whom I have not beaten in our previous One Wall Doubles matches, at the One Wall Nationals. We have not met in singles, in the Four Wall. I did win a doubles match at this tournament, against him. He has a National, One Wall Singles Title, in our age group. This is a player I would love to beat. His reputation for playing hard and winning, is well established. His Four Wall game is a little suspect, as far as I am concerned. I am not really sure how well versed he is, on the high volley game aspect. There is no way for him to know my singles game strategy, either.

As it turns to game time, these exact things surface; my plan to keep him back deep in the court, is working well. He has planned to score on my "weakness" up front; this turns out to be an error. My game, in that aspect, is much improved, by those great games with the champs I competed with at Coney Island all summer. The first game is mine, 21- 10, before he can adjust. The second game, of our best of three match, is much tighter. Mainly, because he has stepped up the effort, in the extreme. It is, dead even, at 8 points each. Everything about my game is fine and I feel confident in a few ways. The match is far from over, when my opponent is forced to take a sudden step forward by an unexpected shot of mine, that is sneaking too low in front of him. He falls forward, hearing the classic noise and feeling as if something "hit" the back of his leg. Many have felt and heard this indication of a sudden injury; all experience the same sensation of being hit or even shot in the back of the leg. After a short time, he acknowledges, it is over. He has likely torn his calf muscle and torn tendons. I advance "On to the Finals" on Sunday. I will get a plaque, first or second place. That's good.

As it turns out for the Sunday Final, I will have a familiar opponent. My friend, Byron, from the YMCA, has won his way to the Final. He and I, have literally played 100 singles games at our Y, and more doubles games against each other! There is little we do not know, about the others game play.

We play an early match, on a bitter cold, Sunday morning. I am relaxed and fit. Getting an early start from my home, for the forty minute trip to Syosset, will insure a calm and thorough warm up. My son, Mike, is in the finals of his events, too. Great day.

As I near the exit for the Syosset area, on the Long Island Expressway, they close the road! I get off, in fine shape and make a wrong turn, immediately taking me on thirty minutes of unnecessary wandering. This upsets me, terrifically.

Making my arrival does make me feel a little better. I am not overly anxious about the outcome of my match. I have a chance to win, being bigger, stronger, and in some ways more skillful. My opponent is, five years younger, AND ran the NYC marathon this year. He also, has a real serving advantage, being able to snap hooks off the bounce to initiate each service point , confusing my anticipation and approach. The ball literally takes a bad bounce from the spin imparted on his serves. This would be a very interesting match to analyze, skill wise. This will not matter, if I cannot avoid the conditioning factor. The guy is tireless, and I suffer fatique in all serious matches. My friend Jared, gave me a simple tactic to manage my breathe, and dodge the oxygen debt that paralyzes me.

In the rules of handball, each player has ten seconds to regain their positions, after each point. At that time, the ref can push the pace. So, when you are serving; Jared said, "Take some time." This I did.

Just before entering for the first game of the match, a nice friend of mine began to tell me about a recent operation. Of course, my attention was divided, to say the least. Maybe it shows my weak attitude that, this four minute "Spinal Surgery Seminar," distracted me, badly. The ref said, "are you ready?" I said, "sure", got on the court and lost the first game without breaking a sweat. Nothing to be done, but take it as a good warmup. I caught myself up, with a new set of gloves, no liners, and got back on the court quick, to warm up for the second game. Hitting the ball as hard as I could, my heart got busy and I felt ready. Played the second game in control, made my serves, killed my set-up shots, kept hitting the ball deep in the court, and my opponent off balance. Still, it was a tight deal with Byrons' abilities, I won the second game, 21- 17. and forced the third, and deciding, eleven point, tie breaker.

Best of all, no oxygen debt, at all. Thanks to my coach, I controlled the pace, my opponent, and my breath.

Entering the Tiebreaker action, my mindset was exactly what is needed. In the moment, prepared, and in action, present, the world outside - non existent.

The play of the second game was soon recalled between us, in the shorter more critical exchanges of the third. A small lead, taken early through Byron's errors, held steady. I was ahead 4-1, then 8-5, then 10-7 and Out! Made the matchpoint, Eleven with Byron at eight. Our referee, Jimmy, and a few friends, complimented our play. It was some of the best play, that either of us could muster. Byron was a good sport, as usual.

When the dust settled, this was a pretty big deal for me. There was a good chance this victory might never occur. Sitting on a couch, outside the glass walled court, where my son was in the middle of the Open Championship Match with Tyree, I saw him look over to me, with the question. The question he has asked me, so often before.

This time, Thumbs up, Thumbs up, Mike. I Won! For a Moment, I had only one thought.

My son has a Great Smile!

Chapter Q: Secrets of 88

Keeping a Secret, 88 Style.   NYC 2014,   July, the Afternoon on the Bench.

Atlantic Avenue, it is not near the ocean.   Me, I am in the same park where my
Dad and Mom once played, and danced, and ice skated, as kids in Ozone Park.   Ozone
Park is...not...near the upper atmosphere; it's named after train emissions. Of course,
the Park isn't named Ozone.   The name is "London Plane Park", after a kinda' tree.
The chances that anyone will ever call it 'London Plane' is the same as the chance
that Vinnie will tell his friend's secret.

The Park is called 88, because it borders 88 th Street on one side. I have played a
couple of Handball games, and sit with the boys on the bench at 88, listening and
chirping a bit myself.   I get to talk quite a bit. The crew has adopted me completely,
though I am old as hell.

Two of the regulars have been discussing various aspects of jail and prison life. This
topic is not unusual, and almost anything is accepted among friends here. The two
have shared the stories of three years on Burglary upstate, and a brother that is
doing seventeen years in the Federal System.   We also covered some new designer
synth drug info.   My part in this is nodding and laughing. These are the good guys.
I truly feel completely at home with them, in this place; they accept me as well,
even though, I've not had an arrest. These things are not critical, and no reason to
start judging people. We boys.

Sitting to my left is Vinnie, who is a well educated High School teacher. He is
waiting for winners on the Doubles Money Game. That means, when the game
presently being played, and bet upon, on the Handball court is finished, his turn to
participate in a two versus two match, likely against the winning team, and bet, will
occur. He is also anxiously awaiting the arrival of his partner, to play the doubles
match coming up. These two always play together, they are quiet and good quality
players. His friend is a taller guy, with long arms and a big smile. 88 Money games can
get a mite raucous, or even out of control, but Vinny and his friend rarely do anything
stupid

They're nice guys, in fact. Vinny is really shaky about the friend's lateness, and I, straightout , ask him, "what's the matter?" He says, "My friend has a secret" and "I don't want to tell everyone."

"Come on, man! What is the deal, you can tell me." "Mike, He is a Doctor and he is on Call."

Once that soaked in, I laughed, but I never told, you can't have people knowing that sort of "thing" at 88.

Chapter R: Don't Mention It

The day is Monday, The weather has changed.   I should go fishing.

   Took the spinning rod down to Jamaica Bay, to check the Bluefish run.   Bluefish are tough predators; when they are tiny, they call them snappers. When the get big, they are Choppers; They bite everything, early and often. They feed in schools at the surface, driving the baitfish right into the air. The seagulls will always tell you where the Blitz is on.

   Charles Park is my favorite spot on the Bay. The fishing is not the best, but the park is a nice place for passing a bit of time, away from the mundane life, here in Queens. I have always been called to the water, and seldom fail to reap the spirit lifting energy of the shore.

   The trip south on Cross Bay Boulevard is quick, the last stretch to the Park is through a nice area called Howard Beach. The Bay is very calm because the Channel to the Atlantic is so far away. You can walk a semi-circle from East to West on a scrubby shoreline facing the Bay and, left to right, you will see: Kennedy Airport, The Railroad Bridge, The Wildlife preserve, and as you reach the western shore: The Crossbay Bridge, with Manhattan in the farthest background.

   Today, with the wind traveling over the Airport and toward Manhattan, I had to pick the western shore for casting my lure.   Casting into the wind is, like tugging on superman's cape, you don't mess around with the hawk. As I began snapping the rod forward and releasing the line, the water was pretty quiet. After only a couple of casts, I had a few hits on the moving lure, not the usual smash of a big blue, but the bounce of the size called "Cocktail Blues", around a pound or two.   At the same time, I was distracted by the appearance of "Ospreys" to the south. The kind that cost millions and have fixed wings, that can be rotated, making them like Choppers.   These are not too unusual in the area between JFK and the Skyline of the City. With the upcoming celebrity fest, the security forces are drilling hard. They are fascinating, with their ability to change prop angles and fly slowly. My mind began to drift. I thought of Obama, and the Pope.   NYC is always having some company fly in. The Jet traffic coming over my head from JFK, heading west,   picked up,   and got loud.   Another cast brought a piece of seaweed, the Airliner overhead, turned toward the City, at a altitude that made think of the Twin Towers.   You could see them, from this beach, once. I watched the curve of the flight path slowly veer to the south, across the

Rockaway Peninsula, where an Airliner once went down in Belle Harbor. I wrapped it up and hit the road.

  Today, the Bay could not hold my mind. The fishing was No Good.

  I went to 88, and played handball, me and Randy won all our games. He goes fishing at Charles Park, too.   I didn't mention seaweed.

Chapter S: Cu Chi Sandwich and a Side

Oct. 1970, Stand Down, Infantry Holiday from missions. Days of the week mean nothing.

I have been "in country" nine months. Most of those days and nights, in the jungle, Mostly sleeping on the ground. Mostly, humping my food in my rucksack. Mostly miserable.

Today, I am in Cu Chi, a big base camp, with a PX and a mess hall. In just a few days, the 25TH Infantry is going home. Maybe one or two more missions, and we will disband. Right now, we get a break, two days of stand-down. Pretty soon I am high, drunk and high. I got a package from home. Canned baloney, I got some fresh bread, eating my sandwich in my platoon's hooch. NICE.

Bang-! One shot, we are Way in the middle of a basecamp, I'm shocked, and stoned, and angry !

I hear some voices, people are running, Medic ! I didn't want to hear that. Not going to spoil my party, crap, I hesitate, but I go. You have to GO. Always. They call you "Doc".

Down the company area, I go, to the first platoon hooch. Looking inside I see this:

Some trooper is on the floor, bunch of troops around him, I haven't yet got in the circle, when I realize . . . this is a suicide attempt! One shot to the chest, with an M-16. One medic is already there and the Battalion Doctor, he has a finger stuck, directly in the wound. I am disgusted, not by the gore, but by the idea of this jackass spoiling my sandwich, which was still in my hand.

I walked away, never regretted it, either. Really, I was past caring. It was his business, anyway. OH, yes, the M-16 is an automatic weapon. It will fire, five rounds, in a second. Some guys said I was wrong, who the hell did they think I was ? You can't care, I didn't , cause I couldn't. The guy survived, thought you might care.

This was the beginning and the end of this as far as I was concerned and I wrote it just that way.

I had regarded the Rear area of Cu Chi as a place of sanity, compared to the Boonies.

The story was meant to splay my emotional numbness for all to see and was written forty years after my tour. So, in that sense it was more than closed, I didn't care about this guy at the time and I wasn't about to feign any renewed compassion.

NOW, forty six years later, the story grows legs and runs into me face first. I remembered something about a Murder that occured in Cu Chi, the murder of a Donut Dolly, an American Girl supporting the troops as USO workers do. At the time of this incident, I was so convinced that I was crazy that I doubted everything about it. Cu Chi went crazy over it. Horrid as it was, it had nothing to do with me. Curious to see exactly what had occurred, I searched 'Online' and found a detailed account of the entire affair, including the investigation and suspects. Already chilled to be brought back to this unsettling incident, I realized that one of these guys was an Infantry man from my Unit. Incredibly, the article announced he had failed an attempted suicide. YES, that guy !

I quit the investigating, there and then. The connection just overwhelmed me. There was more to the story, of course. You can search Donut Dolly Online and follow the suspects, if you like. I couldn't help thinking of the family of the girl and how any mention of it would hurt.

This was very hard to write.

Made in the USA
Middletown, DE
23 April 2020